Simply Beethoven

Simply Beethoven

LEON PLANTINGA

SIMPLY CHARLY
NEW YORK

Copyright © 2020 by Leon Plantinga

Cover Illustration by José Ramos
Cover Design by Scarlett Rugers

All rights reserved. No part of this publication may be reproduced, distributed, or transmitted in any form or by any means, including photocopying, recording, or other electronic or mechanical methods, without the prior written permission of the publisher, except in the case of brief quotations embodied in critical reviews and certain other noncommercial uses permitted by copyright law. For permission requests, write to the publisher at the address below.

permissions@simplycharly.com

ISBN: 978-1-943657-64-3

Brought to you by http://simplycharly.com

Contents

	Praise for *Simply Beethoven*	vii
	Other *Great Lives*	ix
	Series Editor's Foreword	x
	Preface	xi
	Introduction	1
1.	The Beginning	5
2.	Beethoven in Vienna: The First Years, 1792-1800	20
3.	Into the New Century, 1800-05	38
4.	Scaling the Heights, 1806-1809	58
5.	Difficult Times, 1809-11	73
6.	Distraction and Coping: 1812-15	91
7.	1816-1820: More Difficulties	109
8.	Adversity and Triumph, 1821-24	124
9.	Struggle and Culmination, 1825-1827	149
10.	Beethoven's Legacy	173
	Sources	179
	Suggested Reading	180
	About the Author	182
	A Word from the Publisher	183

Praise for *Simply Beethoven*

"*Simply Beethoven* is a brief and eminently readable introduction to the life and works of the revered composer. Plantinga offers the layman reliable information based on his many years as a renowned scholar of the musical world of late-eighteenth and nineteenth-century Europe. This book taps into his long and vast experience as a musicologist and educator, bringing to life the spirit of Beethoven and the turbulent times that stood as the backdrop of his extraordinary creative life. A must-read for lovers of Beethoven seeking a short and reliable introduction to history's most powerfully influential composer."

–David Benjamin Levy, author of *Beethoven: The Ninth Symphony* and Professor of Music, Wake Forest University

"A succinct, insightful synthesis, presented in colorful but precise prose, by the dean of Beethoven studies. The many little-known primary source descriptions of Beethoven are themselves worth the price of this book. If you want to learn about the life and art of Beethoven, Plantinga's offering is by far the most efficient and pleasurable book available."

–Craig Wright, author of *The Hidden Habits of Genius* and Professor of Music, Yale University

"Leon Plantinga presents the ever-inspiring story of Beethoven's life, music, and legacy with imagination and verve, including a wealth of colorfully telling details that keep the pages turning."

–Scott Burnham, Graduate Center, City University of New York

"An eminently accessible traversal of Beethoven's life and principal works, enlightening and consistently entertaining. It affords the layperson a perspective laced with erudition but free of jargon. Highly recommended."

—**Robert Levin, pianist and Emeritus Professor of Music, Harvard University**

"This is an elegant, delightful, concise, and richly informative introduction to Beethoven, the man and his music, written by a distinguished scholar whose breadth of learning and measured judgment are present on every page."

—**Leon Botstein, music director and principal conductor of the American Symphony Orchestra and president of Bard College**

"This is a fine introduction for the non-specialist by an eminent specialist. Professor Plantinga, author of the definitive study of Beethoven's piano concertos, has done a masterful job synthesizing the vast scholarship on Beethoven and making it accessible to the general reader."

—**Stephen Hinton, Avalon Foundation Professor in the Humanities, Stanford University**

Other *Great Lives*

Simply Austen by Joan Klingel Ray
Simply Beckett by Katherine Weiss
Simply Chekhov by Carol Apollonio
Simply Chomsky by Raphael Salkie
Simply Chopin by William Smialek
Simply Darwin by Michael Ruse
Simply Descartes by Kurt Smith
Simply Dickens by Paul Schlicke
Simply Dirac by Helge Kragh
Simply Einstein by Jimena Canales
Simply Eliot by Joseph Maddrey
Simply Euler by Robert E. Bradley
Simply Faulkner by Philip Weinstein
Simply Fitzgerald by Kim Moreland
Simply Freud by Stephen Frosh
Simply Gödel by Richard Tieszen
Simply Hegel by Robert L. Wicks
Simply Hitchcock by David Sterritt
Simply Joyce by Margot Norris
Simply Machiavelli by Robert Fredona
Simply Napoleon by J. David Markham & Matthew Zarzeczny
Simply Nietzsche by Peter Kail
Simply Proust by Jack Jordan
Simply Riemann by Jeremy Gray
Simply Sartre by David Detmer
Simply Tolstoy by Donna Tussing Orwin
Simply Stravinsky by Pieter van den Toorn
Simply Turing by Michael Olinick
Simply Wagner by Thomas S. Grey
Simply Wittgenstein by James C. Klagge

Series Editor's Foreword

Simply Charly's "Great Lives" series offers brief but authoritative introductions to the world's most influential people—scientists, artists, writers, economists, and other historical figures whose contributions have had a meaningful and enduring impact on our society.

Each book provides an illuminating look at the works, ideas, personal lives, and the legacies these individuals left behind, also shedding light on the thought processes, specific events, and experiences that led these remarkable people to their groundbreaking discoveries or other achievements. Additionally, every volume explores various challenges they had to face and overcome to make history in their respective fields, as well as the little-known character traits, quirks, strengths, and frailties, myths, and controversies that sometimes surrounded these personalities.

Our authors are prominent scholars and other top experts who have dedicated their careers to exploring each facet of their subjects' work and personal lives.

Unlike many other works that are merely descriptions of the major milestones in a person's life, the "Great Lives" series goes above and beyond the standard format and content. It brings substance, depth, and clarity to the sometimes-complex lives and works of history's most powerful and influential people.

We hope that by exploring this series, readers will not only gain new knowledge and understanding of what drove these geniuses, but also find inspiration for their own lives. Isn't this what a great book is supposed to do?

Charles Carlini, Simply Charly
New York City

Preface

In this book, I aim to present the famed German composer Ludwig van Beethoven (1770-1827) in the context of his own time and place. Beethoven's Europe was in perpetual tumult; as a young man, he witnessed the French Revolution and the Napoleonic conquests that followed. In fact, Napoleon twice invaded and occupied Vienna, where Beethoven lived at the time, with distinct consequences for the composer's career. Then came the effort to restore order after Napoleon's defeat at Waterloo in 1815, with the resultant stifling regime under the Austrian Chancellor Klemens von Metternich. Despite all such turmoil, Beethoven pursued his career in Vienna to the end.

He also struggled with personal demons: progressive hearing loss, perpetual illness, repeated disappointment in love. But in the face of all these impediments, he produced a body of music that brought him unprecedented fame in his own time and a central place in all succeeding repertories of classical music.

I hope to give a straightforward account of this composer's colorful life, and to show something of the nature of his achievement by discussing some of his major compositions, their construction and effect, without resorting to technical language. I have listed at the head of each chapter the compositions that I describe in some detail.[1]

Various friends have contributed to this endeavor; it is a pleasure to acknowledge their help. Prominent among them are people working in the Yale Music Library who have indulged me well beyond the line of duty; they include Karl Schrom, Kathy Mansi, Richard Boursy, Suzanne Eggleston Lovejoy, and the library's direc-

---

1. All quotations are taken from the list of Sources at the end of the book.

tor, Ruthann McTyre. Other colleagues who have lent me an ear and offered advice are Craig Wright and Hannah Lash. I thank my editor in this project, Helena Bachmann, for her careful attention to the text. But I owe the greatest debt to my wife, Ellen Ryerson, for whose constant support (and red pencil) I will always be grateful.

Leon Plantinga
New Haven, CT

Introduction

Although Beethoven died in 1827, his music continues to absorb and move us. His symphonies, concertos, sonatas, and string quartets stand solidly at the center of the classical instrumental repertory. And this music, though without words, speaks to us eloquently of ideas, aspirations, and notions such as heroism, triumph, death and lament, freedom, and joy. The man himself remains a captivating figure: fiery-tempered, suspicious but given to generous impulses, eccentric in the extreme, unkempt, alternating between despair over his mounting deafness and resolve to overcome its effects; for most of his adult life he was perpetually in love but unlucky in its realization.

This vivid life unfolded amid the social and intellectual tumult surrounding the French Revolution and the Europe-wide disruption of the ensuing Napoleonic saga. Beethoven's and Napoleon's careers intersected directly in Vienna during two periods, both times to the composer's detriment. The first time, the Napoleonic invasion of Vienna in 1805 disrupted the premiere of Beethoven's only opera, "Fidelio." The second French occupation of the city, in 1809, ended a satisfying financial arrangement Beethoven had made with his aristocratic supporters, and it marked the beginning of a months-long period when the composer, in his own words, "produced very little coherent work, at most a fragment here and there." When Napoleon finally disappeared from the scene in 1815, Beethoven had to come to terms with the suffocating Restoration that followed—the "Metternich regime," essentially a police state centered in the city where he lived.

Bad health plagued Beethoven throughout his adult life: he suffered constantly from colitis, recurrent bouts with bronchitis, and innumerable local infections. But the central burden of his life, seemingly a prohibitive condition for a musician, was deafness. First evident around 1797 when he was 26, this affliction continued to worsen until about 1814, when Beethoven was, for all practical purposes, totally deaf. Added to this in his later years was the drama surrounding Beethoven's ill-conceived and plainly disastrous guardianship of his nephew Karl: a poignant late-life tale played out just as he marshaled his artistic energy for that final astonishing creative surge that produced the Ninth Symphony, the *Missa solemnis*, and the late string quartets.

Whatever obstacles he faced, Beethoven became the first composer to achieve great international celebrity during his own lifetime. He managed this just at the beginning of a profound shift in how music functioned in European society. By degrees, Beethoven and his followers pivoted from a dependence on the support of well-to-do patrons, with known tastes, to address an emergent public of uncertain preferences. Beginning in his middle years, Beethoven managed to work delicately poised between these two very different modes of operation: accepting commissions from aristocratic admirers but never entering their employ, and reserving the right eventually to publish these commissioned works for his own profit.

Beethoven also navigated skillfully in a chaotic publishing world. In the absence of international copyright regulations, music publishers in various countries routinely put out pirated editions for which the composer received nothing. At other times, they colluded in obtaining new works, each paying only a part of what the composer asked. But the high demand for Beethoven's music allowed him to enforce a novel arrangement to overcome such obstacles: simultaneous publication. He would offer a composition to publishers in Vienna, Paris, and London, for example, stipulating that they all release their publication on the same day—and each pay the composer his fee.

Another feature of the musical environment in Beethoven's time, particularly in Europe's largest cities, was that emerging institution, the public concert with its new audiences. London led the way with several established concert series featuring professional musicians. In Beethoven's Vienna, however, things were less organized: the composer himself usually had to initiate the event, arrange for a location (sometimes it was only a large restaurant), conscript musicians, schedule rehearsals, and take care of publicity and the printing of programs. Many of Beethoven's best-known works were first heard at concerts he and his cohorts laboriously put together. One mammoth event of this kind in 1808, four hours long, featured the premieres of four major works: the Fifth and Sixth Symphonies, the Fourth Piano Concerto, and the Choral Fantasy.

Beethoven began his career as an ambitious performer on a musical instrument, the pianoforte which was itself an innovation of the period. Two basic varieties of pianos existed in the late 18th century: one with a light, delicate mechanism made in Austria and Germany, the other, with a more robust action and sound, from England and France. Beethoven played both, but, as we might expect from a musician with hearing problems, came to prefer those with the stronger sound—which piano makers in both Paris and London obligingly sent him as gifts. The piano in Beethoven's time—and partly because of his example—evolved from functioning (like the harpsichord) mainly as an accompanying and teaching instrument, to serving as a professional solo instrument as well; it was now often heard in the drawing rooms of aristocratic homes and on the concert stage in that new genre, the piano concerto.

We have a remarkably rich and detailed written record of Beethoven's life. Responding to his growing celebrity, several of his friends and associates left accounts of their interactions with him. Among these were three, Franz Wegeler, Ferdinand Ries, and Gerhard von Breuning, whose attachment to Beethoven began when the composer still lived in his native Bonn. In Vienna, there was Ignaz von Seyfried and Anton Schindler, the latter a kind of servant/assistant in Beethoven's later years who provided many long-familiar anecdotes about the composer (but, as we have recently discovered, Schindler had a disconcerting habit of distorting the record to make himself look better).

As Beethoven's stock rose, recipients of his letters began to save them. And he himself was a compulsive saver. The preliminary sketches he habitually made for his compositions, most of them preserved in some 70 sketchbooks, went with him as he restlessly moved from one apartment to the next in Vienna; some of the sketch leaves he had brought with him from Bonn in 1792 were still at hand when he died. There were also the "conversation books" of his later deaf years: packets of paper upon which his interlocutors scribbled down what they had to say, and to which Beethoven occasionally added his own comments. These too he saved, thus leaving generations of Beethoven biographers a unique source—often both puzzling and informative. The aging Beethoven cut a singular figure in the streets of Vienna: sketch leaves (for jotting down any musical idea that might occur to him while he walked) protruding from one pocket of his long black coat, and a pencil and wad of paper from the other, in case he met a friend along the way.

The present account of this man's colorful life and his memorable work starts at the beginning, in Bonn, in 1770.

1. The Beginning

*R*eaders may wish to listen to the following work of Beethoven, discussed in this chapter:

Cantata on the Death of Joseph II, WoO 87

Beethoven was born into a family of musicians active at the Electoral court of Bonn in mid-December 1770.

At the time, Bonn was a smallish town of about 10,000 inhabitants, situated on the left bank of the Rhine, some 15 miles south of Cologne and just north and across the river from the picturesque *Siebengebirge* ("seven hills"), a tourist attraction then and now. The center of activity in the town was the court, presided over by an Elector (or *Kurfürst*)—one of the seven princes of the German realms entitled to cast ballots for the election of successive Holy Roman Emperors. Electors also held an ecclesiastical office; all four Electors in Bonn in the 18th century were also Archbishops of Cologne, the local see.

The main site of the court's activities was an imposing palace that has now become the central building of the University of Bonn. Nearby were the handsome Rathaus, or city hall, a marketplace, and streets of neatly tended houses where many employees of the court, including the Beethovens, lived within easy walking distance of their work.

One aspect of court life the Electors took very seriously was music; they cultivated all three of its traditional branches, music for the church, the chamber (or concert room), and the theater. Musical activities routinely absorbed a large share of the court's budget; even ordinary church services at court featured a full complement of musicians. Many of these musicians also performed in the concerts of the court orchestra—quite a large one by contemporary standards and known for the excellence of its leading players.

The Bonn court also frequently hosted visiting opera troupes, and, toward the end of the century, maintained its own resident opera company. They mounted a full schedule of current French and Italian works, with the addition of local German operas on subjects from everyday life called *Singspiele*.

In 1733, the Elector Clemens August brought to the court a fine young bass singer from Liège, one Ludwig van Beethoven (the "van" testifies to his family's Flemish-speaking background), who soon after his arrival married a young woman from the area. They had a son, Johann, whom the father promptly trained as a musician. Johann, too, eventually became a singer at court; but as his father rose in the ranks to Kapellmeister (supervisor of all the court's musical activities), Johann sank progressively into alcoholism and indolence. He also married a woman from the area, Maria Magdalena Keverich. Their first surviving child (three others died before his birth), named after his grandfather, grew up to become the composer Beethoven.

The family assumed that this son, too, would become a musician and made rigorous, if often rather haphazard, arrangements for his training. More than one neighbor recalled seeing the small child standing before the piano on a footstool, weeping. And in a well-known story from a reliable witness, we hear about father Johann, coming home with the boy's teacher after a long night of drinking, rousing him for a lesson that would last until dawn. At about this time an observer living in the same house described young Ludwig as "short of stature, broad shoulders, short neck, large head, round nose, dark brown complexion; he always bent forward slightly when he walked. In the house, he was called *der Spagnol* (the Spaniard)." Several who knew Beethoven as a child recalled him as rather withdrawn, largely absorbed in his own solitary pursuits.

Poverty and strife marked Beethoven's childhood. His mainly dysfunctional father took no responsibility for his son except for his musical training, and in this, he was both harshly demanding and critical of any show of ingenuity or originality. The young Beethoven spent most of his waking hours on keyboard lessons and practice, and, for a time, with violin and viola study as well; his teachers were all musicians at court.

Father Johann tried twice to present Ludwig as a child prodigy like Mozart, first taking young Ludwig to play in nearby Coblenz at the age of eight. Two years later, in a similar effort, Ludwig and his mother sailed down the Rhine to Holland. The weather was cold; she later recalled holding the boy's feet in her lap to keep them from frost-bite. Neither of these ventures seems to have been much of a success.

Beethoven in later years always spoke very warmly of his mother, whom acquaintances described as a quiet, serious, long-suffering woman who bore the entire responsibility of caring for the family—while enduring an almost uninterrupted series of pregnancies. Only three of her children lived to adulthood, of whom the composer was the oldest. Contemporaries reported that young Ludwig also clung to his grandfather the *Kapellmeister*, whom Beethoven later remembered with great admiration. But the association could not have been a lasting consolation for him: the elder Ludwig suffered a debilitating stroke when the boy was two, dying a year later.

For a time, young Beethoven attended an elementary Latin school in Bonn. But his general schooling ended before his 11th birthday, which for those of Beethoven's social class was not uncommon. Perhaps to compensate for his lack of higher education, Ludwig became an earnest auto-didact in later years. Filled with a simple reverence for Homer, Immanuel Kant, and Friedrich Schiller, he accumulated a considerable—though rather ill-assorted—library. Still, traces of an inadequate elementary education remained with him for life. For example, he never seemed to have learned simple multiplication; as a man in his 40s, he calculated his compensation for publications of his music by repeating the amount per copy in a single long column and adding it up.

Beethoven's teacher C. G. Neefe

Meanwhile, Ludwig made great strides forward as a musician. In the autumn of 1779, shortly before he turned nine, young Beethoven's musical prospects improved dramatically with the arrival at court of an admirable musician from Leipzig, schooled in the traditions of the Bach family, Christian Gottlob Neefe. Neefe had been a student of Johann Adam Hiller, a stalwart proponent of musical craft based on strict contrapuntal writing in the Bachian tradition.

Neefe came to Bonn at the age of 31 as a composer and director of *Singspiele* for the Grossmann theater company, then in residence at the court; but his advanced abilities as a keyboard player soon led to his appointment as court organist as well. Beethoven quickly became his eager pupil, and Neefe supplanted the boy's father as Ludwig's principal music teacher. And as early as mid-1782, when Neefe's operatic duties took him elsewhere, the 11-year-old Beethoven took over his teacher's duties as organist for church services at court.

In a communication to a musical journal, J. Cramer's *Magazin der Musik*, in the spring of 1783, Neefe registered the first public notice of young Beethoven's musical prowess:

> a boy of eleven years and of most promising talent. He plays the clavier very skillfully and with power, reads at sight very well, and—to put it in a nutshell—he plays chiefly *The Well-Tempered Clavier* of Sebastian Bach, which Herr Neefe put into his hands . . . So far as his duties permitted, Herr Neefe has also given him instruction in thorough-bass. He is now training him in composition and for his encouragement has had nine variations for the pianoforte, written by him on a march—by Ernst Christoph Dressler—engraved at Mannheim . . . He would surely become a second Wolfgang Amadeus Mozart were he to continue as he has begun.

Neefe's emphasis on the works of Bach in Beethoven's musical curriculum, particularly on the 48 Preludes and Fugues of *The Well Tempered Clavier*, was something of a position statement. By the time young Ludwig was mastering these works in the 1770s, for most of Europe Johann Sebastian Bach's rigorous music represented all that was pedantic and old-fashioned; one prominent Leipzig critic called such music *schwülstig*, or "turgid." The style in fashion in the second half of the 18th century, called *galant*, was much simpler—often little more than a tune and its accompaniment laid out in predictable rhythmic patterns. The music of Mozart and Joseph Haydn, each in its own way, constitutes a marvelous adaptation of this reigning style. But Neefe, coming from Leipzig, Bach's city, brought with him a veneration for the intricacy of the stricter, more complex, older style of music, and made it an important building block in Beethoven's training.

Despite his preferences for music of the past, Neefe fit in well with Bonn's more progressive intellectual and political currents. He participated actively as a member of the Illuminati, a branch of Freemasonry openly espousing the populist, anti-clerical political positions that were beginning to roil Europe, especially France. And after the Bonn court banned that group, Neefe participated in the local *Lesegesellschaft* ("reading society") that pushed similar ideas in a more prudent fashion.

During the 1780s, under the rather progressive Emperor Joseph II, the Austrian empire was generally receptive to at least the more moderate versions of secular Enlightenment thought. But Bonn, situated on its western edge, closer to Paris than to Vienna, was a center of more radical strains of liberalism. A new university, established there in 1784, soon became a hotbed of liberal politics. A lecturer on theology and classical literature there, Eulogius Schneider, emerged in the following decade as a fire-brand supporter of the French Revolution. (He ended his days, ironically, as its victim, dying in Paris in 1794 by the guillotine.) Beethoven spent his early years surrounded by this heady mix of liberalism, revolutionary politics, and Enlightenment optimism. These forces shaped his thought for life.

In his 1783 report on Beethoven's progress, Neefe mentioned that he had arranged for the publication of some music by his young charge: nine variations on a march by E. C. Dressler, a singer and writer about music whom Neefe had known in Leipzig. This is Beethoven's earliest known composition. Variations for keyboard were at that time distinctly the province of amateur players; Beethoven's youthful effort—particularly in the left-hand part—is distinctly more inventive and more difficult than was expected in such music. And in a couple of places, flashes of originality signal the special talent of this 11-year-old.

In the following three years, Beethoven produced a thin stream of new works, all solo piano pieces or Lieder (i.e. secular German songs), including three piano sonatas published in late 1783: the so-called *Kurfürstensonaten*, dedicated to the ruling Elector (or Kurfürst) Maximilian Friedrich. These sonatas (identified as "WoO 47," i.e. "work without opus no. 47"), though at points distinctly juvenile, reflect the ambitions of a gifted young musician. The opening movement of the second sonata, in F minor, dramatic and portentous, recalls Haydn's "Sturm und Drang" symphonies—particularly the first movement of his "Farewell" Symphony of the previous decade. This music also has a certain individual sound to it: a clear foretaste of Beethoven's special talent for drama in minor keys.

In 1785, the 14-year-old composed some of the most substantial instrumental music of his Bonn years: three spacious piano quartets (for piano, violin, viola, and cello), each in three movements. These works show a distinct advance in coherence and invention over the sonatas written two years earlier. Beethoven's own favorable view of this music became clear a decade later as he adopted several ideas from these quartets for his newest compositions. The best-known instance of this is in the first piano sonata he equipped with an opus number (thus conferring upon it a certain canonic status), the Sonata Op. 2 no. 1 in F minor. The exquisite Adagio of this work, composed in 1795, is a deft reshaping of a quartet movement he had written as a teenager.

At the beginning of 1784, the 13-year-old musician, until now an unpaid apprentice at court, applied for a regular position as assistant court organist, whose duties included playing for church services, as well as accompanying at concerts and opera performances. Having received the appointment, Beethoven was entitled to wear the official livery of the court musician—including a sword on special occasions. But momentous events in Bonn were soon to disrupt all his plans. In February 1784, the Rhine overflowed, flooding much of the town. The Beethovens lived right on the river, and the family was forced to make a hasty evacuation to temporary quarters where they remained for the rest of the year. Then two months later, the Elector at the Bonn court, Maximilian Friedrich, suddenly died, precipitating the dissolution of all artistic and social functions at court until a successor could be installed.

To the musicians of Bonn, the new Elector, Maximilian Franz, looked like a good choice. As the youngest son of Empress Maria Theresa and Emperor Franz I, and younger brother of the current emperor, Joseph II, he came with the best possible connections to Vienna's Imperial Court. He played violin and viola, and—though hugely corpulent—loved to dance. He was a passionate devoté of music and theater, and a passionate admirer of Mozart—unaware that the latter, in a letter of 1781, had written about him that "Stupidity oozes out of his eyes."

Maximilian Franz immediately ordered full reports and financial accounts of all court functions, including musical ones. As a result, young Beethoven now received a small salary and, for the only time in his life, became a paid participant in the musical patronage system.

Friends in Bonn

Beethoven's work and social activities both revolved around the court, and some of the associations he made there lasted for most of his life. Several of his friends were musicians or sons of musicians.

Chief among them was Anton Reicha, exactly Beethoven's age, who in 1785 arrived in Bonn with his musician father, newly appointed as cellist and leader of the court orchestra. The younger Reicha (who later recalled that he and Beethoven had been, "like Orestes and Pylades, constant companions") became an estimable composer and writer on music. He later continued his association with Beethoven in Vienna. In 1808, he moved to Paris, where he wrote influential treatises on music history and theory, and eventually counted among his pupils Hector Berlioz, Franz Liszt, and César Franck.

Then there was the Von Breuning family. Helena von Breuning, the widowed mother of four children, welcomed Ludwig into her household, and he apparently spent a good deal of time there. Her daughter Eleonore became his piano pupil and—in a pattern that we shall see oft-repeated—the object of his affections. Her son Stephan and Beethoven formed a sometimes fractious friendship that, as in the case of Beethoven and Reicha, continued in Vienna. With various of these friends, Beethoven played chamber music; the houses where he spent time in Bonn were well known for the fine sounds wafted into the neighborhood.

Two other Bonn natives had a lasting significance in the composer's life: the physician Franz Wegeler, some five years older than Beethoven, and Ferdinand Ries, a pianist and composer 14 years his junior. Shortly after Beethoven moved to Vienna in 1792 Wegeler followed him there, where, he later recalled, "there was hardly a day when we did not see one another." In 1802, Wegeler married Beethoven's former pupil and early love Eleanore von Breuning and settled into a distinguished medical career in Coblenz.

Ries, son of a long-term violinist at court, also moved to Vienna in about 1801 where he became Beethoven's piano pupil ("three lessons a week," he reported, and "the accuracy on which he insists surpasses belief"). In 1813 Ries moved to London, where his performances and teaching gained the esteem of the city's musical world, and where he served as Beethoven's loyal agent in dealings with the British. Wegeler and Ries together published an extensive and generally reliable collection of reminiscences of Beethoven (*Biographische Notizen über Ludwig van Beethoven*, 1838).

A report on the musical forces at court that Elector Maximilian Franz commissioned in 1784 took note of Johann van Beethoven, tenor, "age 44 . . . has three sons living in the electorate, age 13, 10, and 8 years, who are studying music . . . Johann Beethoven has a very stale voice, has been long in service, very impoverished." Somewhat more hopeful is the note on his son Ludwig: "is of good capability, still young, of good and quiet deportment, and impoverished." But on occasion the boy Beethoven seemed to attract the special attention of the new ruler. Something of a row erupted in the court chapel during Holy Week of 1785 when Ludwig, accompanying at the piano a solo singer in the plainchant Lamentations of Jeremiah, successfully set about to "unhorse" him with unexpected and obscure harmonies. The singer lodged a furious complaint with the Elector, who duly commanded a "simpler accompaniment" (but, some said, he was privately much amused).

First visit to Vienna

The Elector's estimate of Beethoven was favorable enough that in April 1787 he granted the 16-year-old leave from court duties for a trip to Vienna, apparently with expenses paid. So that spring this still rather provincial young musician had his first taste of one of the world's grandest capitals.

Since the mid-17th century, Vienna was the seat of the hugely expanded Hapsburg dynasty and a powerful magnet for Europe's musicians. Italian and French opera were regularly performed at the theater in the Hofburg (the central court complex); German theater and opera could be heard at Schönnbrunn, the summer palace on the outskirts of the city, and at smaller theaters scattered about town. In the grand houses that lined the busy streets near the center of the city, music was the standard entertainment; some even maintained small standing orchestras. But from the beginning of Maria Theresa's reign, we also see the gradual emergence in Vienna of that new social entity, a "musical public"—some seats at the opera and concerts were now available to anyone, of whatever rank, for the price of a ticket.

In arranging this trip to Vienna, both the Elector and Beethoven apparently had in mind the prospect of study with Mozart, who was then at the pinnacle of his career. He had just returned from a month-long stay in Prague, flush with the success of *Figaro* the previous spring, and now armed with a new opera commission that was to result, the following autumn, in *Don Giovanni*.

While the details of Beethoven's stay in Vienna are hard to trace, the trip was overall surely a disappointment. It is fairly clear that he met Mozart and heard him play piano. His later verdict on that performance, "a fine but choppy—*zerhackt*—way of playing . . . no *ligato*," reminds us that in the 1780s the piano was still a very new instrument; Mozart's playing surely reflected a keyboard technique formed at the harpsichord. But Beethoven had played the piano from early childhood and was determinedly fashioning a new and distinctive approach to the instrument.

Unfortunately, after less than three weeks in Vienna, Beethoven was abruptly called back to Bonn by news of his mother's illness. In a letter to an acquaintance in Augsburg, where he had stopped on the way home, he wrote, "The nearer I came to my native city, the more frequent were the letters from my father urging me to travel with all possible speed." He was still able to spend nearly three months with his mother before she died, in July 1787, at the age of 40; the cause, Beethoven reported, was consumption, the 18th-century term for tuberculosis.

As his father became increasingly dysfunctional, his mother's death left Beethoven, at 16, effectively in charge of the household of four. Weighed down by his new responsibilities, amid grinding poverty, melancholy, and a bodily affliction he described as "asthma, which may, I fear, develop into consumption," he settled back into his old life as a fledgling court musician. During this time of crisis, the young man's circle of friends and associates in Bonn lent a helping hand. Ferdinand Ries's father Franz, the leading violinist at court, provided some financial support, and the Breuning family was a source of solace. Then, about six months after Beethoven's mother died, a new figure destined to play a large role in the young musician's life appeared in Bonn: Count Ferdinand Ernst Gabriel Waldstein, younger son of a highly-placed Bohemian family well connected with various strands of European nobility. At age 26, Waldstein came to Bonn as a novitiate knight of the Teutonic Order, a mystical religious organization with roots reaching back to the 13th century; it had been founded for military protection of Christians on pilgrimages to the Holy Land, but now had become largely a ceremonial presence. As the Elector Maximilian Franz was a Grand Master of the Order, Bonn was an important center of its activities.

Waldstein was a skilled amateur musician—younger sons of the nobility, unencumbered by the cares of succession and inheritance, often had ample leisure time for such pursuits—and he became a constant companion of the Elector. He performed minor diplomatic duties for the court and played a pivotal role in its musical life. Beethoven's friend Wegeler recalled that Waldstein was "the first, and most important Maecenas of Beethoven," freely providing him both money and advice. In 1788-9, Waldstein took part in forming a new local troupe of performers for theater and opera at court. This undertaking involved virtually all its musicians, including Beethoven, as a regular violist in the opera orchestra. Thus, from an early age, in both concerts and opera, Beethoven learned about the workings of the orchestra from the best possible vantage point: the inside.

About three years later, on February 20, 1790, a momentous event in Vienna affected all the members of the Bonn court. The Emperor of the Austro-Hungarian Empire, Joseph II, died after a 10-year reign. By this time, he was widely unpopular; the aristocracy had always resented his populist leanings, and the austerity measures required by his failed military adventures squeezed everyone. Still, for many in Bonn, this standard-bearer of the Enlightenment remained a shining hero.

The Joseph Cantata

When news of his death reached the town on February 24, the Reading Society launched plans for a memorial celebration the following month. The local firebrand liberal Eulogius Schneider, who was to deliver the eulogy, urged that the program also include a new cantata. A young theology student accordingly produced a text, and Beethoven was chosen to compose the music, to be known as the Joseph Cantata. But he failed to finish on time; the piece was not performed, and the music remained unknown until the score resurfaced in the 1880s. (The same thing happened for the elevation ceremony of Joseph II's successor, Leopold II, later the same year: Beethoven's cantata again arrived too late.)

The unperformed Joseph Cantata, scored for solo voices, choir, and orchestra, is a startling achievement. Up to this time, as far as we know, Beethoven had had no experience managing such extensive resources. But despite a sometimes-embarrassing text (overdone pathos verging on bathos), the piece comes across as a convincing little musical drama. Sentiments of Enlightenment liberalism popular in Bonn abound. "A monster called Fanaticism rose out of the depths of hell" becomes an agitated accompanied recitative (i.e. the sort of speech/song routinely used in opera at points of alarm or dread). The expected aria follows: "Then came Joseph who, with the strength of God, destroyed the raging beast." The fanaticism it says Joseph demolished was of the religious sort; and, it is true, he had closed monastic institutions across the land.

In a later soprano aria ("Then mankind rose to the light"), Beethoven wrote a noble soaring melody that, 15 years later, he reused at a similar point of exaltation ("O God, what a moment") at the climactic close of his only opera, *Fidelio*. The Joseph Cantata stands as a solid milestone in the growth of the young composer's powers. After the reemergence of this music in the 1880s, Johannes Brahms exclaimed, "Even if there were no name on the title page none other could be imagined–it is Beethoven through and through."

Beethoven's commission to compose two major pieces for performance at the Bonn court–although the performances never happened–was an exceptional event. From the beginning, his growth as a composer and solo player was largely removed from the old-style courtly system in which he was raised. He surely benefitted from the attentions of those with high connections at court, particularly those of Count Waldstein. And he reportedly played piano occasionally in the great homes of such people. His salaried position at court enabled him (though just barely) to support himself and, towards the end, his younger brothers as well.

But in his growth as a composer and performer, he apparently made his way with precious little official support. It is a mistake to think of Beethoven's position as a liveried musician in Bonn as comparable, say, to Mozart's situation in Salzburg, where in the corresponding part of his career he too held a post as court organist. Mozart's music was regularly performed at court, often under his own direction. During his time in Bonn, Beethoven compiled a list of some 40 compositions; we know of only one, the *Ritterballet* ("Knightly Ballet") of 1791, that was performed at court–and in that case, he was not even named as the composer. Thus, Beethoven was not at all a usual product of the 18th-century patronage system; he pursued his real career mainly in his spare time.

Travel with Court Musicians

In autumn of 1791, the Teutonic Order held a month-long conclave in its capital, Mergentheim (now Bad Mergentheim), some 300 kilometers from Bonn, on the Tauber River. Not wishing to be deprived of their usual entertainments, the Elector and his retinue arranged for the transport of most of the court's musicians to Mergentheim (in addition, for evenings without concerts, he engaged several traveling opera troupes). Thus, Beethoven and his fellow players set off on a three-week boat trip southward against the stiff current of the Rhine (they would have turned east into the Main River at Mainz and then into its tributary, the Tauber).

The musicians treated this outing as an occasion for a good deal of high-spirited revelry and foolishness. But the trip also held some solid benefit for Beethoven's career. During a stopover at the Electoral summer palace at Aschaffenburg, he listened intently to the performance of Abbé Johann F. X. Sterkel, one of the most revered pianists of the time, and then demonstrated to Sterkel his own surpassing powers of improvisation.

Then, at Mergentheim, he met Carl Ludwig Junker, a prominent, if somewhat erratic, music critic, who published a glowing tribute to the Bonn players. He singled out Beethoven for special praise: "one of the greatest of pianists . . . his style of treating the instrument is very different from the usual manner." This was perhaps the earliest sign that a contemporary of Beethoven's saw something of the true singularity of this rising star.

Some months earlier, on Christmas day, 1790, the court had celebrated a visit from the foremost musical luminary of the time, Joseph Haydn, who stopped off on his way to London in the company of his handler, Johann Peter Salomon (a native of Bonn). The Bonn musicians performed one of Haydn's masses in the court chapel and arranged a banquet for him afterward. It is not clear whether Haydn and Beethoven actually met on this occasion. But upon Haydn's return to Vienna in July 1792, he once more stopped in Bonn, and this time surely interacted with the younger composer. (Wegeler recalls that Beethoven showed Haydn the Joseph Cantata). But more importantly, this was the occasion when Beethoven's superiors at court—mainly Count Waldstein, it appears, as the Elector was out of town—arranged for the young musician to travel to Vienna to become Haydn's pupil.

The powers at the court probably did not act out of pure magnanimity. Napoleon's armies were making their way northward down the Rhine; by October, Mainz and most of the left bank were in French hands. The Elector and his court packed up their valuables and prepared to leave town. The danger abated somewhat, and they remained in Bonn, but this time of high anxiety led them to hold in abeyance many activities at court, including musical ones. It was a good time for Beethoven to take his leave of absence.

However paltry the Bonn court's official support of Beethoven's aspirations had been, the Elector agreed to foot the bill—very modestly, in Beethoven's opinion—for his travel to the capital city and his upkeep there. The assumption was that, after further training in Vienna, Beethoven, like other young musicians before him, would return to a resettled Bonn court, better equipped to serve. As preparations were made for his move, Beethoven kept a memorandum book in which his friends and supporters recorded their thoughts. Eleanore von Breuning's note quoted the admired poet Johann Gottfried Herder:

> Friendship with a good friend
>
> Grows like the evening shadow
>
> Till the setting sun of life.

Waldstein's entry has been much quoted:

> Dear Beethoven!
>
> You are going to Vienna to fulfill your
>
> long-frustrated wishes . . . With the aid of assiduous labor
>
> you shall receive Mozart's spirit from Haydn's hands.

On November 2, 1792, Beethoven climbed into a post-coach for the trip to Vienna, where he was to remain for the rest of his life.

2. Beethoven in Vienna: The First Years, 1792-1800

*W*orks discussed in the present chapter are:

Piano Trios, Op. 1

Piano Variations on "Venni Amore" by V. Righini, WoO 65

Piano Concerto No. 1, Op. 15

Piano Sonatas Op. 2, nos. 1 and 3

According to a commonly used travel guide of the time, if Beethoven left Bonn at 6:00 AM by post-coach (the fastest available mode of travel), he could stop for dinner in the city of Koblenz at 3:00 PM, arriving in Frankfurt-am-Main the next morning. He would face at least four more such grueling round-the-clock journeys to reach Vienna.

And his travels were full of peril: by 1792, Austria and France were at war, and French revolutionary troops were in control of much of the western part of Beethoven's route. According to his diary, he tipped the driver at Koblenz, as "the fellow drove us . . . right through the Hessian army going like the devil." When he arrived in Frankfurt, the city had been under French control for a month. Still, on November 10, some eight days after leaving Bonn, he arrived safely in the Imperial city.

Vienna presented a rich cultural mix. It lay on the frontiers of Germanic, Slavic, and Hungarian populations, and on ancient crossroads for river and land trade. There Beethoven would hear around him many languages and dialects, including French widely spoken among the aristocracy, and Italian commonly used by musicians (one remembers Mozart's fluent conversations with his Italian colleagues). But in late 1792, Vienna, like all the empire, was in a state of political agitation. The progressive measures of Joseph II—expanding the freedoms of ordinary citizens, regular washing of city streets in summer, severely limiting the political influence of the Catholic clergy, granting new liberties to Protestants and Jews—were gradually rescinded as the revolution in Paris struck fear into the hearts of the privileged classes.

Leopold II, Joseph's successor, had come to the imperial crown with a record of enlightened rule as the Grand Duke of Tuscany. But he lived only until the spring of 1792 when his eldest (and reportedly least impressive) son assumed the throne as Franz II. Even before he took office, Franz had helped lay the foundations of the police state that was to hold sway in the Austrian dominions for all of Beethoven's life in Vienna. Once in power, Franz firmly established the "Metternich System," a master plan for social control named for Beethoven's conservative fellow Rhinelander Prince Clemens Metternich, foreign minister and later chancellor of the Austrian dominions.

What Franz and his advisors most feared were conspiratorial societies of liberal or pro-French sentiment. Two years after Beethoven's arrival in Vienna, police ferreted out what they saw as a nest of Jacobins—the most extreme faction among French revolutionaries. Some received sentences of death, and some, life imprisonment. The regime also instituted a pervasive system of censorship that extended to musical productions: in 1797, suspecting possible revolutionary implications, they banned the publication of a composition called *Friedens-symphonie* ("Peace Symphony"). Thus, when the 21-year-old Beethoven moved to Vienna, he exchanged an environment that openly encouraged his liberal and humanitarian impulses for one that would see them as suspect, even dangerous.

Still, on the surface life in Vienna—particularly in its love of public pleasures—seemed to go on much as before. People living in the city's typically small apartments spent time freely in pubs and coffeehouses; of the latter, there were over 70 in Vienna proper and about 45 in the suburbs, according to a 1793 estimate. And there were public amusements of many kinds. In 1775, Joseph II (as regent) had opened an expansive public park, the Augarten; it offered tree-lined avenues for strolling, as well as venues for dining and musical performances. In 1784, a certain Herr Stuewer had caused a sensation with his daring hot-air balloon flight from the park. But not all activities were benign; several theaters were devoted to the gruesome spectacle of animal-baiting. But in the mid-1790s, Franz II, in one of his few constructive acts, forbade it.

Beethoven joined a steady stream of hopeful students, artists, and musicians arriving each year in this walled capital of the Austro-Hungarian Empire, still the epicenter of theater, opera, art, and music for all of Eastern Europe. Live theater, with or without music, was the entertainment of choice for the nobility and better-situated bourgeoisie. The two court theaters—the Burgtheater in the palace complex itself, and the nearby Kärthnerthortheater (Theater at the Kärntner Gate)—both presented plays and operas. The operas were overwhelmingly Italian; the big hit of 1792 was *Il Matrimonio segreto* by Domenico Cimarosa. Two private suburban theaters, the Josephstadt and the Leopoldstadt, provided somewhat lower-brow drama in German, often with music. A fifth theater, one that was to figure prominently in Beethoven's career, started out in 1787 as the Theater auf der Wieden (Mozart's *Magic Flute* had premiered there just a year before Beethoven's arrival). In 1801 its director, Emanuel Schikaneder, moved it into a spacious new building and gave it a new name, Theater an der Wien.

Concert life in Vienna

But unlike London, which at this time featured two highly popular competing public concert series in large venues (where Haydn was just now the big sensation), Vienna had only a thin roster of concerts open to all comers. The Burgtheater offered the closest approximation to a concert series: four annual performances for the benefit of widows and orphans of deceased musicians—two at Christmas and two at Easter. There was, in fact, no dedicated public concert hall. The theaters occasionally hosted public concerts for most of the second half of the 18th century. After the model of the *Concert spirituel* of Paris, concerts in Vienna occurred primarily during Advent and Lent, when dramatic entertainments were forbidden.

Concerts also sometimes occurred in two halls in the court complex that were mainly used for dancing, the Grosser Redoutensaal and Kleiner Redoutensaal (the "large and small dance halls"), especially during the restricted seasons when dancing, like drama, was banned. Other concerts were held in restaurants and private dance halls. Two such venues, the restaurant Trattnerhof and the casino-like Mehlgrube, had been the setting for Mozart's subscription concert series of 1784 and 1785. After the mid-1780s, performances of various sorts also took place in the Augarten, either out-of-doors, or in the hall of the Gärtengebaüde ("Gardenbuilding").

The ambiance at these events was, as an advertisement in a local newspaper suggested, casual: "In the adjoining rooms gaming tables for all types of sociable games will be held in readiness, and each person will be served with all sorts of refreshments according to his wish."

When a musician like Mozart or Haydn wished to present his newest music in a public concert, (or as it was then called, an "academy"), he had to make all the preparations himself: reserve a space, seek police permission, conscript the other musicians, arrange for publicity, copy parts, and schedule a rehearsal (there was usually just one). The orchestra was most often composed of a mixture of amateur and professional players, the latter mainly among the wind players. Here is a newspaper announcement of such a concert from December 1795:

> This coming Friday, the 18th of this month, Herr Kapellmeister Haydn will give a grand musical academy in the small Redoutensaal, in which Mad. Tomeoni and Herr Monbelli will sing, Herr van Beethoven will play a concerto of his

composition on the pianoforte; and the three grand symphonies that the Herr Kapellmeister prepared during his latest sojourn in London, not yet heard here, will be performed.

Such an announcement was of course directed toward the public at large in the hope of selling enough tickets to make a profit. But the social structure in Vienna still required a composer-performer like Beethoven to invest most of his energies elsewhere: in private musical events under aristocratic patronage—an arrangement he had grown quite accustomed to in Bonn. At the time of his arrival, the scale of private music performances in Vienna was on the decline. Few of the great houses still maintained orchestras; by the mid-1790s about the only one remaining was that of Prince Joseph von Schwarzenberg in his fine palace in the Mehlmarkt, where Haydn's oratorios *The Creation* and *The Seasons* had first been performed. Less exalted aristocratic homes might have had a string quartet in residence, a small wind ensemble, or just a couple of servants who played an instrument in their spare time.

Nonetheless, as Beethoven settled in Vienna, ambitious musical events in grand houses, sometimes even with (newly-assembled) orchestras and chorus, were still a prominent part of the musical landscape. They took place in residences bearing the noble names of eastern European vintage we have come to associate with his own: Prince Nikolay Galitzin, Prince Karl Lichnowsky, the two Princes Lobkowitz, Prince Joseph von Schwarzenberg, and Prince Ferdinand Kinsky.

Beethoven's feelings had always been conflicted about the aristocracy and his place in their midst. But soon after his arrival, his diary reports, he set about outfitting himself with some of the necessities for life among the nobility: "Black silk stockings, winter silk stockings, boots;" he even took dancing lessons. Whether these measures proved effective is open to speculation. A young pianist who had moved to Vienna shortly after Beethoven, Elisabeth von Bernhard (née Kissow) recalled seeing "Haydn and [Antonio] Salieri sitting on a sofa . . . both carefully dressed in the old-fashioned way with wig, shoes, and silk stockings . . ." But Beethoven, she observed, "was small and common-looking, with an ugly, red, pock-marked face. His hair was quite dark and hung disheveled about his face . . . he spoke in a strong dialect and in a rather common way."

Beethoven moved into a small room in the attic of a house near the center of Vienna, brought in a piano, and began his life in the big city. But he had barely settled in when solemn news reached him from Bonn: his father had died in mid-December. (For the occasion the Elector offered a joke: "The revenues from the liquor excise have suffered a loss . . .)." Beethoven petitioned the Bonn Court for his father's vacated salary, and was granted half of the amount, somewhat relieving his financial problems.

Study with Haydn

Beethoven began lessons with Haydn almost immediately after his arrival in Vienna. His course of study closely followed established tradition, which entailed writing strict Renaissance-style counterpoint based on a treatise from 1725, the *Gradus ad Parnassum* of the Viennese composer J. J. Fux. Beethoven would start with a melody from church plainchant, add a second melodic line above (later on, appending a third and fourth) governed by intricate rules. Then Haydn would correct the exercise—often rather carelessly. The pupil chafed under the restrictions of this sort of instruction, and, according to Ferdinand Ries's later recollection, Beethoven claimed he "never learned a thing from it."

But Beethoven continued his lessons with Haydn for about a year, until the latter left for his second London sojourn at the beginning of 1794. And he even invented a ruse to improve Haydn's impressions of his work: he secretly gave his completed exercises first to a more experienced composer, Johann Schenk, who corrected them. After copying the corrections, Beethoven submitted the work to Haydn. Still, Beethoven must have seen some value in this detailed, nuts-

and-bolts practice of the craft: after Haydn's departure, he immediately switched to another teacher, the established Vienna musical pedagogue Johann Albrechtsberger, who offered more of the same instruction. What Mozart had learned from his father in early childhood, Beethoven was earnestly trying to master in his early 20s.

Beethoven cultivated that other sector of musical prowess, his virtuoso piano playing, entirely on his own; he did so well that he was soon considered the best pianist in the city. An oft-repeated story recalls Beethoven's competition with the local composer and pianist Abbé Joseph Gelinek. Gelinek, the story goes, once met the father of Carl Czerny (later Beethoven's faithful student) on the street. "Where to?" the father inquired. "I am asked to measure myself against a young pianist who is just arrived; I'll work him over." A few days later they met again. "Well, how did it go?" "Ah, he is no man—he's a devil. And how he improvises!"

Such an encounter would likely have taken place in a private home, where music for piano (except piano concertos) was most often heard. And various aristocrats in the city loved to stage competitions between pianists; Beethoven participated in—and won—quite a few in his earlier years in Vienna. The competiveness, not to say paranoia, he felt toward other pianists in the city emerged in his 1794 letter to his erstwhile love in Bonn, Eleonore von Breuning. Enclosing his recent set of piano and violin variations on Mozart's aria from *The Marriage of Figaro*, "Se vuol ballare" ("If you wish to dance"), he explained that some fiercely difficult passages in the piano part were there for a strategic purpose:

> Another reason I had was to embarrass the local pianoforte masters. Many of them are my deadly enemies, and I wanted to revenge myself on them, knowing that once in a while somebody would ask them to play the variations, and they would make a sorry show of it.

The attic room where Beethoven first lived in Vienna was in the residence of Prince Karl Lichnowsky, one of the city's leading aristocratic patrons of music. (Lichnowsky was also famous for leading a degenerate life, fathering several illegitimate children and finally succumbing to syphilis.) Himself an eager musician, Lichnowsky had been a friend and benefactor of Mozart, and became Beethoven's foremost early supporter. He soon moved the young musician out of that attic room into his own spacious quarters. In his home he maintained a string quartet made up of very young players; two of them, the violinist Ignaz Schuppanzigh and the cellist Nikolaus Kraft, became Beethoven's long-time associates and collaborators.

The Piano Trios, Op. 1

Every Friday morning Lichnowsky held a house concert where Beethoven, along with other local musicians, became both a participant and listener. At one of these events, with Haydn present, Beethoven presented his three newly finished piano trios (multi-movement compositions for piano, violin, and cello) that he later published as Op. 1, with a dedication to Lichnowsky. The other musicians found this music splendid and strikingly original. Haydn generally approved, but took exception to the third trio of the set—the one in C-minor that we now recognize as most clearly "Beethovenian"—and advised him not to publish it. This astonished and angered the young composer; he liked that piece the best, and proceeded to publish it along with the other two.

That this music should appear as Beethoven's Opus 1 meant something. Beginning in the 18th century, instrumental music routinely appeared in print with opus numbers as a rough means of identification and a guide to chronology. But often things went wrong: publishers sometimes introduced a good bit of confusion—particularly if more than one publisher was involved, a frequent occurrence in the absence of international copyright regulations. Thus, opus numbers for Mozart's works are next to useless; hence the catalogue with those familiar "K" numbers, originally compiled by Ludwig Koechel.

In Haydn's case, we rely on opus numbers only for the string quartets.

But already early in his career, Beethoven seemed to entertain some notion of a "canon" of his works; he attached opus numbers only to music he considered worthy of inclusion therein, and he did his best to keep the numbers straight. His designation of those trios, premiered at Lichnowsky's, as "Opus 1," shows that Beethoven thought this music marked the true start of his career as a composer. And he had a point. The Op. 1 Trios have a technical assurance and a vividness of expression hard to find in his earlier music.

Piano trios, like all the big pieces of this period written for piano plus other instruments, descended directly from that earlier genre, very popular among amateur musicians, the "accompanied keyboard sonata." As a result, their piano parts tended to dominate the texture imperiously, sometimes even allowing for performance as piano solos. Haydn's piano trios, even the late ones, clearly reflect this lineage. Beethoven's Opus 1 departed from that tradition, making the string players, if not quite equal partners with the pianist, at least essential, active accomplices.

Opus 1 strikes the listener as an able, inventive exercise in late 18th-century high classical style, with eruptions of startling individuality around the edges. The recurring main theme of the Presto finale of the first trio, in E♭, enters with far-flung agile leaps in the piano, later slyly mimicked by the strings. The following Trio in G major starts with a rhetorical, portentous slow introduction that resolves magically into a cheerful, untroubled Allegro. The first and last movements of the third trio (the one about which Haydn had his doubts) abound with the drive and dark passion of Beethoven's personal "C-minor" manner (most familiar to us, perhaps, from the first movement of the Fifth Symphony); an island of relief from all that turbulence, a calm, sunny Andante with variations, comes in the middle.

A new audience

During the latter part of the 18th century, an entirely new social phenomenon took shape in Europe's principal cities: an expanding contingent of mainly middle-class people with increasing economic and political power that coalesced to form a "public." This public had certain collective needs, desires, and ideas—the expression "public opinion" appeared in several languages at this time. Opera performances and concerts open to anyone with the price of a ticket proliferated, suggesting the emergence of a "musical public." But there were other signs as well. As increasing numbers of people indulged their interest in the arts, they began to do what only aristocrats had done in years past: make music in their homes.

Beethoven's main contact with a musical public during his later period in Bonn and first years in Vienna came through publication of his keyboard music. From the beginning, there was a clear distinction between what he wrote for amateurs to play at home and what he intended for his own performances. Most of his early sets of piano variations, a favorite genre among recreational pianists, were clearly intended for the amateur market. One example is the Variations from 1795 on the duet "Nel cor piu non mi sento" ("I no longer feel in my heart") from Giovanni Paisiello's opera *La Molinara*. Wegeler recounted this story: one evening, Beethoven attended a performance of *La Molinara*, together with a lady "of standing" in her box. She told him she owned a set of variations on that duet, but had misplaced them. So later that evening Beethoven composed six variations on the theme, sending them to her in the morning with a note, "They are so easy, the lady will surely be able to play them at sight."

The Variations on an arietta of Vincenzo Righini, "Venni amore," are quite another matter. This is evidently the music Beethoven had played in Mergentheim back in 1791 to impress the Abbé Sterkel. Later he performed it in Vienna as well, and published it in a much-revised version as late as 1804. The theme is an ingenuous, almost absurdly simple ditty, perfectly symmetrical, 8 measures + 8 measures. Beethoven wrote 24 variations of growing complexity on the theme, some scaling previously unknown heights of keyboard virtuosity. One variation requires an extreme crossing of hands (and arms!) while playing fast scales in both hands; another features rapid simultaneous scales in "double thirds" (i.e., each hand in effect plays two scales a third apart). Interestingly, Beethoven appeared to distinguish a work such as this, designed largely to display his astonishing abilities as a pianist, from his central work as a composer. Apparently, he did not consider it part of his "canon" and gave it no opus number (it is now designated WoO 65).

Meanwhile, developments back in Bonn were conspiring to make Vienna Beethoven's permanent home. The onset of the Terror in Paris in 1793 raised high alarm—Marie Antoinette, guillotined in October of that year, was, after all, the Elector Max Franz's older sister. And during the next year, as French armies advanced eastward, principals of the court always stood ready to leave. The fateful day came in October 1794: the French marched in, and the Elector and some of his retinue fled—first to Muenster, then to Frankfurt, followed by Mergentheim and other places. Though for a few years the peripatetic Max Franz and his entourage hoped for a return home, the Bonn court was a thing of the past. Beethoven too had assumed that he would one day return to the court; now there was nothing there worth returning to.

In March and December of 1795, Beethoven twice took part in that worthy new institution, the public concert: in March he appeared in one of the regular benefit concerts for the families of deceased musicians, and the following December in a concert given by Haydn, newly returned from his triumphs in London. Concerts in those days always served up varied fare: usually they started with a big ensemble piece such as a symphony (or a movement of one); next came assorted vocal and instrumental numbers in rough alternation. Arias from recently performed operas were especially popular. Instrumental soloists typically presented concertos, often of their own composition, and that is what Beethoven performed in these concerts. We do not know for certain, but most likely it was the much-revised Concerto in B♭, Op. 19, and the Concerto in C major, Op. 15, that he played on those two evenings.

The Concerto in B♭ had been around for quite some time: Beethoven had played it in private settings in both Bonn and Vienna, each time making revisions, at least one as drastic as replacement of a whole movement. He once explained that he "held his concertos back" from publication until he had gotten all the mileage he could out of them in performance. This concerto still seemed like a distinctly earlier work, a rather rough imitation of Mozart's masterpieces in the genre, when he offered it to a Viennese publisher in 1801 with an apology: "A concerto for pianoforte, which, it is true, I do not claim is one of my best . . . At the same time it would not disgrace you to engrave this concerto."

The First Piano Concerto

If the B♭ Concerto shows Beethoven's struggle toward mastery of the "high galant" or "classical" style long since achieved by Haydn and Mozart, in the best pieces of 1794-5 he had already left that stage behind. By the time he was able to join this august company, he had already struck out in directions of his own. The Concerto in C, Op. 15 (known as his "First Concerto" because it was published in 1800, a year before the B♭ concerto) is a good example of his progress. This work follows the tradition of orchestral pieces in C major with trumpets and drums (i.e. tympani); since the Renaissance the province of royalty, these instruments were regularly associated with festiveness and exaltation.

These instruments—and the key of C major—had also long been associated with things military. The concerto's quiet, tense, stiffly regular opening motive in the strings invokes a distant infantry march—much like Leporello's "Nott'e giorno faticar" at the beginning of *Don Giovanni*. Then, the march is suddenly near, fortissimo, all trumpets-and-drums splendor. When the piano finally enters, it sounds at first almost irrelevant—as if the soloist's thoughts were still elsewhere and needed to be drawn into the business at hand. But presently the piano swings into the central action to engage in fine dialogue with the other instruments. Yet throughout the movement we may sense a certain difference between the priorities of the two participants: the orchestra favors straightforward, often exclamatory statement, while the soloist leans toward a certain caution and circumspection.

After this bracing first movement comes a warm, reflective Adagio leading to a spirited rondo finale. In this rondo, the ever-returning main theme, as with most rondos from the period, recalls the contredans (the name deriving from the English "country dance"). Such movements make a point of ingenuousness: with regular, straightforward rhythms and predictable internal repetitions meant to invoke the innocence and joys of country life.

In this connection, we might recall another passage from *Don Giovanni*: the peasant scene in Act I where Zerlina, Masetto, and their rural friends enter, singing and dancing. This lively music proceeds in untroubled even note-values until in the chorus ("che sara, la la la ra"), when the mask of naivety slips: a sophisticated little rhythmic turn suggests a peasant's dance finishing off with, say, a stylish little ballet-like pirouette. The themes of Beethoven's rondos usually do something similar. In the First Concerto, the easy rhythmic predictability is amusingly upset when that rondo theme just ploughs on for one bar too long.

Beethoven wrote other remarkable music in 1794-5, notably the three piano sonatas, Op. 2, also first heard at one of Lichnowsky's Friday morning gatherings. Keyboard sonatas at this time were normally directed toward one of two distinct destinations: for performance in private settings by the composer (or sometimes by another accomplished pianist), or, more frequently, for publication and amateur delectation.

For Beethoven, such a distinction hardly existed—he composed virtually no sonatas for amateurs. With a couple of exceptions (the

Sonatas Op. 49 of 1795-7 for example), his earlier piano sonatas were intensely personal vehicles, vividly distinctive in expression, often suggestive of the imaginative flights of their author's keyboard improvisation. The derring-do technical feats in the outer movements of the third Sonata of Op. 2, the almost painfully extended ending of the exquisite Adagio in the first sonata, and the relentless, exhausting running left hand of its finale—all this evokes images of the brash young composer at his own instrument, astonishing and delighting listeners with his new-found powers of expression and execution.

For Beethoven, there was one advantage to the French occupation of Bonn: it drove a number of his old associates to Vienna, sparking the revival of his earlier social life. The physician (and later Beethoven biographer) Franz Wegeler arrived in 1794. Stephan von Breuning, a close friend and brother of his early love Eleanore, came the following year. Both of the composer's younger brothers ended up there as well: Caspar set up shop in Vienna as a music instructor—and, in effect, as Beethoven's personal secretary—in 1794; Johann got a job in an apothecary shop at the end of 1795. (Considerably later, in 1808, Johann opened his own apothecary shop in Linz and accumulated a considerable fortune providing medicines for the occupying French army.) So, Beethoven slipped back comfortably into his old role as the responsible, sometimes overbearing older brother, handing out both advice and, less frequently, money.

Travels outside Vienna

Early in 1796, Beethoven left Vienna on a trip that became his longest absence from the city in all the years he lived there. Just as Mozart had done seven years earlier, he traveled with Prince Lichnowsky to Prague, where he played piano for the city's music-loving aristocratic audiences. In a rather ebullient letter to his brother Johann back in Vienna he wrote:

> In the first place I am getting on well—very well. My art wins for me friends and respect; what more could I want? This time, too, I shall earn considerable money. I shall remain here a few more weeks and then go to Dresden, Leipzig, and Berlin... I hope that you will be more and more pleased with your life in Vienna; but beware the whole guild of wicked women.

Now evidently traveling alone, Beethoven made his way to Dresden, where his performance before the Saxon Electoral Court earned him a golden snuffbox—a fairly standard gift for visiting soloists. Next, after a brief stop in Leipzig, the city of his musical idol J. S. Bach, he traveled on to Berlin, the Prussian capital. There he performed several times at the court of King Frederick Wilhelm II. In addition to the expected display of his famous improvisational wizardry, he played his two new Sonatas for piano and cello, Op. 5, with the court's resident cello virtuoso, Pierre Duport.

These sonatas break completely free of the "accompanied keyboard" mold, presenting the two instruments in an intricate and equal relationship. The second one, in G minor, is a big, complex piece that in the end resolves into an untroubled, rather serene finale. These two sonatas appeared in print the following year with a dedication to the king—himself an enthusiastic amateur cellist.

While in Berlin, Beethoven associated with a number of local musicians, including the pianist Friedrich Himmel (to whom Beethoven attributed only a "pretty talent"). A much more formidable rival pianist there, in his estimation, was the colorful Prince Louis Ferdinand, nephew of the current king; Beethoven once complimented him by saying that his playing sounded not at all like that of a king or a prince.

A central musical organization in the city was the Berlin Singakademie, which mounted performances of oratorios and other pieces for large musical forces under the direction of the composers Karl Friedrich Fasch and Karl Friedrich Zelter (later Felix Mendelssohn's teacher). At one of its performances, Beethoven agreed on the spot to step to the piano and extemporize elaborately on the theme of a fugue just played—and which he had heard for the first time. Before he left the city, Beethoven's aristocratic hosts presented him with another golden snuff-box; but this one was filled with gold coins.

Back in Vienna, Beethoven's life settled into predictable patterns. During most of the year, he lived in the city (changing apartments with astonishing frequency), while in the summers he sought out cooler and less crowded places, often near water, where he could take advantage of long daylight hours to concentrate on his work. His city life was the more varied of the two: he accepted some students, mainly female, and mainly from the ranks of the aristocracy, and he continued to perform at the piano, both in private gatherings and occasionally at public concerts. As more and more of his music appeared in print, Beethoven began to spend more time in—often edgy—correspondence with publishers. Still, on many evenings he could be seen with his friends, almost exclusively male, in one of the many coffeehouses or pubs of Vienna.

During 1796-1797, city residents, especially members of the aristocracy, watched with great anxiety as French military forces led by the upstart general Napoleon Bonaparte advanced through the northern Italian peninsula and the Tyrol region towards Vienna. The local military (always pathetic by comparison) hastily mobilized amid a wave of local patriotism. As Haydn's hymn "God preserve Franz the Emperor" (later given new words, "Deutschland über alles") gained popularity—it was sung regularly before theatrical performances—other composers in the city, including Beethoven, hastened to follow suit. In 1796, he produced "Farewell to the Citizens of Vienna," written to cheer on a volunteer regiment as it marched ceremoniously out of the city, banners flying. The following year he composed "War Song of the Austrians." But such pieces constituted a negligible part of his output in a period of great productivity for Beethoven. In 1796-1797 alone, he finished some 30 compositions; Viennese music publishers eager for his work printed about half of them immediately.

During the latter 1790s, though often edgy and sometimes a bit paranoid in his associations with others, Beethoven formed several close and lasting friendships. Most of his friends, whatever their profession, were also serious amateur musicians. One was Nikolaus Zmeskall von Domanovecs, born in Hungary, and an official in the Hungarian Court Chancellery in Vienna. A fine cellist, he occasionally played at the Friday morning gatherings at Lichnowsky's home, which is likely where he and Beethoven met. The two of them frequently took their midday meal together at the restaurant Zum weissen Schwan ("The Swan"), and Zmeskall often performed useful services for the impractical composer. For example, he carved the quills that Beethoven needed for composing but was unable to make himself. In his letters to Zmeskall, Beethoven often adopted an over-the-top bantering tone that made fun of Zmeskall's official position and his standing in the lower ranks of the Hungarian nobility. One such letter is addressed to "His Highly Well-Well-Bestborn, the Herr von Zmeskall, Imperial and Royal, also Royal-Imperial Court Secretary."

But the most intense friendship Beethoven formed during this period was with Karl Amenda, a clergyman and violinist from Latvia who spent just over a year in Vienna from the spring of 1798 to the summer of 1799. Amenda found employment in the private orchestra of Prince Joseph Franz Lobkowitz and for a time as the teacher of Mozart's children in the home of his widow Constanze. Amenda and Beethoven spent many hours playing chamber music, and could frequently be seen walking the streets of the city together. After family obligations required Amenda to return to Latvia, they kept up a sporadic correspondence until at least 1815. Beethoven wrote of Amenda, probably in 1801, "A thousand times the thought of the best human being I have ever met comes to my mind."

Shortly thereafter, Beethoven confided to Amenda his most momentous personal concern, that central fact of the composer's life—his mounting loss of hearing: "Let me tell you that my most noble faculty, my hearing, has much deteriorated. When you were still with me I felt signs of this and remained silent about it. But now it has grown constantly worse; whether this can ever be corrected only the future can tell."

The only other person with whom Beethoven discussed this disastrous matter at the time was the physician he had known since his boyhood in Bonn, Franz Gerhard Wegeler. Wegeler had fled Bonn in the fall of 1794 as the French army approached and, like many refugees from that city, settled for a time in Vienna. There, he later reported in his reminiscences of the composer, hardly a day passed when he did not see Beethoven. But less than two years later he returned to Bonn, where in 1802 he married Beethoven's early beloved, Eleonore von Breuning. As with Amenda, Beethoven carried on a warm and personal—if intermittent—correspondence with Wegeler long after his departure. It seems that the often-irascible composer's closest personal ties were best carried on from afar, free from the frictions of actual encounters.

In a letter from the summer of 1801, Beethoven wrote to Wegeler of "that jealous demon, my wretched health," particularly his chronic digestive problems and the alarming decline of his hearing. A local physician, he said, prescribed a "strengthening medicine" for his stomach, and almond oil for his hearing—both without effect. Another "medical ass," Beethoven reported, suggested cold baths; a third, more sensibly (Beethoven felt) advised lukewarm Danube baths into which Beethoven was to pour a bottle of "strengthening stuff." This was followed by pills for his stomach and an herbal infusion for his ears. He now felt better and stronger, he said, but his ears "continued to hum and buzz day and night." "I must confess," he continued, "that I lead a miserable life. For almost two years I have ceased to attend any social functions, because I find it impossible to say to people: I am deaf."

3. Into the New Century, 1800-05

*W*orks discussed in the present chapter:

First Symphony, Op. 21

String Quartets, Op. 18, Nos. 3 and 6

Piano Sonata, Op. 31, no. 2

Third Symphony ("Eroica"), Op. 55

Fidelio (*first version of the opera*)

At the beginning of the 19th century, as he approached the age of 30 while struggling with health and hearing problems, Beethoven nevertheless pressed ahead with plans for his first public concert in Vienna. He organized it himself and offered a program consisting mainly of his own works. It took place on April 2, 1800, in the prestigious Burgtheater, the splendid hall next to the Imperial Palace, built by Empress Maria Theresa in the 1740s mainly for the performance of Italian opera (three of Mozart's had premiered there). That Beethoven's concert could command this space signaled his rising stock among the top aristocracy of the city.

The program largely followed contemporary customs. It consisted of a rough alternation of instrumental and vocal numbers: an unidentified Mozart symphony, selections from Haydn's *Creation*; Beethoven's First Piano Concerto with the composer as soloist; two new compositions, his Septet and First Symphony; and—in an individual twist—Beethoven improvising at the piano. The leading musical journal of the time, the *Allgemeine musikalische Zeitung* (General Musical Journal) called the concert "the most interesting in a long time." The journal's only reservations—having to do with some confusion and bad playing by the theater orchestra—stemmed from Beethoven's insistence at the rehearsal on replacing its regular concertmaster-conductor with one of his own choice, with whom the others then refused to play.

For his main appearance as soloist at this Vienna debut, Beethoven chose an older piece—the First Piano Concerto, Op. 15 of 1795—which he had played repeatedly during his travels of 1796 and 1798 to Berlin, Prague, and Bratislava. (He seems to have played it in private at least once in Vienna as well.) One of the two new pieces heard that evening was the Septet, Op. 20, written for four string instruments and three winds. It comes in six movements, in the fashion of the older *divertimento*, a relaxed, sociable sort of instrumental music. This piece, sounding appropriately affable and faintly old-fashioned, scored an immediate hit. For the rest of the 19th century, amateurs played it in a host of arrangements: for piano four hands, piano and various other instruments, as a string quintet, and in various other guises.

The First Symphony

The other new composition on the program presented another story. Here Beethoven ventured onto the territory that was to yield his greatest triumphs, the symphony. But for now, he faced the daunting prospect of competition with the towering masterworks of his fellow Vienna residents, Mozart and Haydn, the latter still present in the city and revered all over Europe. Until now, Beethoven had had only limited experience writing for full orchestra: just the first two piano concertos (where the orchestral writing is by nature much less concentrated), and a couple of aborted attempts at a symphony—a try at a movement in C minor from the early Bonn years and an unfinished symphonic movement in C major he had worked on in 1795-6.

Still, the First Symphony comes across as marvelously assured: a sparkling, engaging work, much in the mold of the late Haydn symphonies, yet with Beethoven's fingerprints in plain sight. Its first movement begins, Haydn-like, with a teasing slow introduction that feints toward one key, then another. Then the movement proper settles down into the sort of energetic, distantly martial-sounding music Beethoven often favored for compositions in C major. (A close relative of this theme introduces the C-major piano concerto heard the same evening). A later, contrasting lyrical section deftly manages an interplay among the winds—flute, oboe, clarinet, bassoon—again sounding like the best of late Haydn.

The following Andante enters as if on tiptoe. Full of engaging imitation among the various instruments, it rises to a certain rhetorical warmth without abandoning its overall air of understatement. Next comes a very fast, exuberant Menuetto. While it resembles the Scherzos in Haydn's later symphonies, this movement exceeds them in bounding energy. Its opening theme skips up the scale with great abandon, but near the top, buffeted by unexpected harmonies, threatens to lose its balance. The finale is a joyful rondo, where the much-awaited return of an infectious main theme, here heard three times, holds center stage. This first symphony showed the relative neophyte Beethoven in full control. In one bold step, he had seemingly joined Haydn and Mozart at the pinnacle of classical instrumental style.

The String Quartets, Op. 18

In another audacious move at the turn of the century, Beethoven challenged the pre-eminence of Haydn and Mozart on a second front: the string quartet. Haydn had essentially invented the string quartet as we think of it: as an ambitious, "elevated" genre, a substantial composition typically in four movements, directed at an informed audience, in which the composer invests his greatest powers of invention and technique.

Mainly under the young Haydn's hands in the 1760s and 1770s, the String Quartet had begun life as one of various genres of "social" music, that is, music normally played in the background as aristocrats talked at social gatherings. It came in various instrumental combinations and with a variety of names, such as divertimento, notturno, or serenade. After publishing four sets of such pieces, called either divertimento or quartet, in his String Quartets Op. 20 (1772), Haydn signaled his plans for the genre by writing the finales as fugues, that is, music in strict imitative counterpoint—a style seen then, and now, as severe, serious, and a bit old fashioned.

Then, in 1782, he put out his Quartets Op. 33, composed, as the printed music announced, in "an altogether new and special manner." Here we see the engaging and mature Haydnesque style emerge: with easy exchanges in informal counterpoint in which any instrument may for the moment carry the melody. Mozart expressed his admiration three years later by publishing his own masterful six string quartets and dedicating them to Haydn.

From 1798 to 1800, Beethoven followed suit, working steadily on the six Quartets, Op. 18, finally publishing them in 1801 in Vienna. This music, like the First Symphony, shows a fairly clear debt to both Haydn and Mozart (in the fifth quartet of the group, in A major, Beethoven apparently modeled his work directly upon Mozart's quartet in the same key in the set dedicated to Haydn). But at many points in this music, Beethoven quite explicitly set out on his own.

The first of the group to be finished, the Quartet No. 3 in D, begins with a movement of studied tranquility. The first violin starts with an expansive first theme, soaring effortlessly upward and gliding back down in unhurried stages. The other instruments (except for the cello) follow suit, establishing an overall languid air for this movement. Later, just before the return of the first theme in the recapitulation, the four instruments, seemingly impatient with all this restraint, belt out an exasperated tattoo of repeated chords at top volume in a foreign key. This is the sort of eruption that earned Beethoven's music its reputation as irrepressible, sometimes even rude. But this brief rant ends abruptly, and the first melody carries on in its quiet way as if nothing had happened.

The slow movement comes across as the most ambitious of the three. Its main theme, earnest and plain-spoken, stretches out over 12 measures and plays an outsized role in the proceedings. An unserious, stiff-legged second idea emerges for a moment but soon yields to the insistent reappearance of the main theme. In the central section of the movement, the development, the four instruments exchange unhurried elaborations of that first theme; it appears in the ever-changing light of shifting keys and new accompaniment figures. Here, and throughout this movement (and, indeed, in these quartets as a whole), Beethoven commits himself to writing real counterpoint—music in which two or more instruments simultaneously play their own coherent melodic lines.

Probably the most memorable movement in these quartets is the finale of the last one. It begins with something quite unexpected in a finale, an Adagio introduction (Haydn and Mozart often wrote slow introductions for first movements, not last ones). And what an introduction it is. Entitled "La Maliconia," (melancholy, gloom), it presents a sober rising melodic line that gives way to agonized dissonant chords, alternating high and low, loud and soft—a convincing musical *cri de coeur*. What this remarkable passage introduces, it turns out, is a distinctly light-hearted Allegretto in even fast notes. But toward the end, this music stops dead, and we hear, once more, the agonized sounds of the Introduction—like memories of a troubling dream intruding upon the ordinary events of the day.

Beethoven was no stranger to melancholy. In November 1801, he wrote another long letter to Wegeler, his trusted friend and medical advisor. Again full of woe about his afflictions, he described treatments for deafness prescribed by his doctors (one was "vesicatories"—something that causes blisters—attached to his arms). But Beethoven also mentioned a certain welcome distraction from his suffering:

> My bad hearing haunted me everywhere like a ghost and I

fled from mankind. I seemed like a misanthrope, and yet am far from being one. This change has been wrought by a dear fascinating girl who loves me and whom I love. There have been few blissful moments within the last two years, and it is the first time I feel that—marriage might bring me happiness. Unfortunately she is not of my station—and just now it would be impossible for me to marry—I must still bustle about a good deal.

That dear, fascinating girl was apparently Julia Guicciardi, whose father, Count Franz Joseph Guicciardi, had assumed a post at the Imperial Court in 1800. Soon thereafter, Julia became Beethoven's piano pupil. Even if the difference in their social station had not presented a barrier to their marriage, the difference between their ages surely would have: when she became his student, Beethoven was almost 31, and Julia was 16. Two years later, Beethoven expressed his lingering feelings for Julia by dedicating the famous "Moonlight" Sonata (Op. 27, No. 2) to her.

That gesture, however, was to no avail: later that year, Julia married Count Wenzel Robert Gallenberg, 19, and moved with him to Naples. Before her departure, according to Beethoven's much later recollection, Julia came to him in tears, but he flatly rejected her advances. Soon after she left with her new husband, Beethoven published two songs (composed some years earlier) that he may have associated with this poignant episode in his life: "Zärtliche Liebe ("Gentle Love"), and "la Partenza" ("The Parting").

In a long-extended summer retreat in 1802, Beethoven spent about six months in Heiligenstadt, a picturesque village with hot springs outside Vienna. He settled into the upper floors of an isolated house outside the village in compliance with his current doctor's recommendation that he "spare his hearing as much as possible." There he remained until the autumn, in October falling into a depressive state that apparently led him to the verge of suicide. He wrote a lengthy and astonishingly rhetorical meditation on his situation; discovered after his death, this document came to be known as the "Heiligenstadt Testament." Purportedly addressed to his brothers, it is also clearly directed toward a much larger audience. Here are some excerpts:

> Oh you men who think I am malevolent, stubborn, or misanthropic, how greatly do you wrong me. You do not know the secret cause that makes me seem that way to you. From childhood on my heart and soul have been full of the tender feeling of good will, and I was ever inclined to accomplish great things. But think, that for 6 years now I have been hopelessly afflicted, made worse by senseless physicians, from year to year deceived by hopes of improvement, finally compelled to face the prospect of a lasting malady (whose cure will take years, or perhaps be impossible).
>
> Though born with a fiery, active temperament, even susceptible to the diversions of society, I was soon compelled to withdraw myself, to live life alone . . . It was impossible for me to say to people, "speak louder, shout, for I am deaf." Ah, how could I possibly admit an infirmity in the one sense which ought to be more acute in me than in others, a sense which I once possessed in the highest perfection? . . .
>
> I sometimes yielded to my desire for companionship. But what a humiliation for me when someone standing next to me heard a flute in the distance and I heard nothing, or someone heard a shepherd singing and again I heard nothing. Such things drove me almost to despair. A little more of that and I would have ended my life—it was only my art that held me back. Ah, it seemed to me impossible to leave the world until I had brought forth all that I felt was within me . . .
>
> That fond hope—which I brought here with me, to be cured to a degree at least—this I must now wholly abandon. As the

leaves of autumn fall and are withered—so likewise has my hope been blighted.

Astonishingly, Beethoven's depression in Heiligenstadt seemed to have little or no effect on his productivity. During his months there he finished his Second Symphony, composed the three piano-violin Sonatas Op. 30, the Bagatelles Op. 33, and at least the first two of the three Piano Sonatas Op 31. Writing many years later, his student Carl Czerny recalled Beethoven's remark from that period: "'I am not satisfied with what I have composed up to now. From now on I intend to embark upon a new path.' Soon thereafter the three sonatas of Op. 31 were published."

The "Tempest" Sonata

This self-assessment has something to be said for it. The works composed in Heiligenstadt, particularly the Sonatas Op. 31, show Beethoven's new assurance in working in a distinctly personal style. Best known of these sonatas is the second one, in D minor. (Beethoven's distinctly unreliable biographer, Anton Schindler, reports that he asked Beethoven about the "meaning" of this piece, to which Beethoven replied, "read Shakespeare's *The Tempest*"—which thus became the sonata's inseparable subtitle.) In this sonata, we see the juxtaposition of vividly contrasting materials in *La Malinconia* raised to a structural principle. At the outset, Beethoven sets diametrically opposed snippets of Largo and Allegro side by side—the one a simple slow-rising arpeggio, the other a nervously agitated stepwise falling figure in the right hand. At first, this sounds distinctly improvisatory—as if Beethoven, sitting at his piano, were experimenting with some bits of ideas in search of a good beginning for a sonata. Then, with the second exchange of these two ideas, the Allegro expands with great energy to usher in the main theme—an organized version of both those snippets.

As the first section of the movement, or "exposition," progresses, we hear three other distinct ideas, each clearly related to the beginning Largo or Allegro, or both. Later we hear these two seminal ideas restated and elaborated as structural markers in what turns out to be an intricately organized movement. When the second movement (Adagio) starts with a slow-rising arpeggio, we are immediately reminded of the piece's beginning; the stepwise answer at a higher pitch confirms that impression as we enter into this leisurely, calming, meditative music. The finale is a bracing moto-perpetuo excursion dominated by an urgent, impatient-sounding main theme; it is again clearly related to those two opening motives of the sonata (the single contrasting theme derives from the second of them). Such an undertaking—to fashion an entire three-movement sonata from a couple of enigmatic ideas presented at the start—was very much an original project. It showed Beethoven's growing conception of a sonata (or a quartet or a symphony) not as an assemblage of diverse movements, but as a coherent whole.

Having survived his personal crisis at Heiligenstadt, Beethoven, now 31, moved back to Vienna and carried on with his astonishing run of productivity. His life was often frenetic. He moved restlessly from one apartment in the city to another, and to outlying areas during summers. Whether in the city or country, and whatever the weather, Beethoven took long calming walks during which he ruminated over his current work, sometimes jotting down ideas on a wad of staff paper he kept in a coat pocket. Finding his music ever more in demand, he was continually in negotiation with publishers in several cities, frequently quarreling with them about publication rights, the accuracy of editions, and his payments. Gradually, his brother Carl took over some of these operations, which often provided some relief, but sometimes led to misunderstanding and confusion.

During these years, Beethoven's method of composing became more routine. He would write down enigmatic snatches of music as a kind of aide-mémoire on single sheets or small gatherings of paper, later entering his ideas in more organized fashion into a sketchbook, where large sections, sometimes whole movements, would gradually take shape. When this process had progressed sufficiently, Beethoven would carefully transfer his sketches into an autograph score, assigning material to the different instruments (for ensemble music) and putting in finishing touches such as phrase and dynamic markings.

Working in sketchbooks was for Beethoven the central act of composing. Some of these books were professionally made, and some he sewed together himself; some were for use at home where he had pens and inkpot, and smaller ones he carried in his pocket (especially later in his career), writing in them with pencil during his walks. Beethoven was a compulsive saver: some sketch materials he brought from Bonn in 1792 were still with him at his death in 1827. An ever-growing stock of sketchbooks went with him as he moved restlessly from one Vienna apartment to the next. About 70 of them have survived until the present day, with the names of their 19th-century owners still attached: Grassnick, Landsberg, Petter—names as well-known to Beethoven scholars as if they were family members.

During the first years of the new century, the Viennese nobility often heard Beethoven's music in their homes, sometimes with the composer himself at the piano. But in the spring of 1803, he arranged, for a second time, to present his works to a public audience. This concert consisted entirely of his own works and took place at the imposing Theater an der Wien, just south of the city walls. It included the First and Second Symphonies, the Third Piano Concerto with himself as soloist, and the first version of his oratorio *Christus am Ölberge* ("Christ on the Mount of Olives"). In those days, concerts in Vienna were typically last-minute affairs. Ferdinand Ries recalled that the main rehearsal for the performance at the Theater an der Wien began at 8 AM on the day of the concert:

> It was a terrible rehearsal, and at half past two everybody was exhausted and more-or-less dissatisfied. Prince Karl Lichnowsky, who attended the rehearsal from the beginning, had sent for bread and butter, clod meat and wine in large

baskets. He pleasantly asked all to help themselves, and this was done with both hands, the result being that good nature was restored. Then the prince requested that the oratorio be rehearsed once more from the beginning, so that it might go well in the evening . . . And so the rehearsal began again. The concert began at 6 o'clock, but was so long that a few pieces were not performed.

That concert and its mammoth rehearsal were, at least, conveniently located for Beethoven, as he had recently taken up lodgings right in the theater, pursuant to a contract he had signed with the management to compose an opera to be performed there. (It was very convenient to have the composer nearby to make changes during rehearsals; Mozart had produced whole new arias under similar circumstances.) That the theater should have turned to Beethoven for an opera might seem remarkable, as the considerable international fame he had by this time derived almost exclusively from his instrumental music. But this was a rather slack period for opera in Vienna. The main attraction on the boards at that moment came from Paris: Luigi Cherubini's *Ladoiska* and *Medea* in German translation. Beethoven agreed to produce an opera, *Vestas Feuer* ("The Fire of Vesta") to a libretto by Emanuel Schikaneder, author of the libretto for Mozart's *The Magic Flute*. But it appears that he composed almost nothing for this opera, leaving only a few desultory sketches from 1803.

Beethoven probably defaulted so conspicuously in his first try at opera because he had other things on his mind, most notably putting the finishing touches on the "Kreutzer" Sonata for piano and violin, Op. 47, and getting started with his Third Symphony, the *Eroica*. As we have noted above, Beethoven inherited a tradition in which sonatas for piano and other instruments were regarded as accompanied keyboard sonatas intended for amateur musicians. But Beethoven's earlier sonatas for piano and violin (there were, finally, to be 10 of them) had steadily elevated both the general heft of such pieces and the importance of the "accompanying" instrument to make it a full partner.

In the "Kreutzer" Sonata, which he described as "similar to a concerto," Beethoven went one step further and wrote an intricate, at points virtuoso, part for the violin. In May of 1803, he played the piece in concert—a very unusual venue for an "accompanied" sonata—with a visiting violin virtuoso from England, George Poltreen Bridgetower. (After a reported quarrel with Bridgetower, Beethoven published the sonata with a dedication to the Parisian violinist Rodolphe Kreutzer—hence its name.)

The *Eroica*

For the summer months of 1803 Beethoven again retreated to the country, this time to a four-room vintner's house near Heiligenstadt, where, surrounded by vineyards and meadows, he concentrated on the composition of his Third Symphony, the "Eroica." Finished by the end of the year, it was truly a watershed work. Heroic even in its physical proportions, it was the longest symphony anyone had written up to that time. It also had no precedents in rhythmic energy, in the scope of its developmental procedures, or in its protracted building of powerful climaxes. It began a series of middle-period works that both inspired and intimidated composers of large-scale instrumental works for the rest of the 19th century and beyond.

The *Eroica* begins with two loud, brusque chords—a dismissive substitute for the Haydnesque slow introduction—and launches directly into a theme that starts in the cellos and migrates upward, followed by a series of vivid contrasting ideas, all striking the listener as fragmentary, one merging into the next. During the central developmental section of the movement, these evasive bits of material reappear, varied and combined in new arrangements. But presently, at the climax of a great tense crescendo, all melody disappears while the whole orchestra hammers away mercilessly at a series of powerful, offbeat, excruciatingly dissonant chords.

All this mayhem then suddenly evaporates as we hear a new, quietly wistful tune in the first oboe. Many have wondered why Beethoven should introduce yet another melodic idea (we've already had about nine of them) this late in the movement. Actually, the bass line played by the cellos provides the key: this is a "filled in" version (i.e. with all the leaps filled in) of the movement's opening idea; the "new idea" is really only a new counterpoint to that very first tune. Finally, toward the end of the movement, everything seems to smooth out as untroubled repetitions of the main theme lead to a climax that sounds like a triumph and maybe reconciliation.

The second movement, entitled *Marcia funebre* (funeral march), has its own unprecedented proportions and weight. Beethoven's contemporary audiences would easily have recognized the expressive intent here: this music resembles the grand dirges performed at funerals for military heroes of the French Revolution and Napoleonic wars. It has compulsively repeated dotted rhythms played at a lugubriously slow tempo, embellished with imitations of military drumrolls—all identifiable traits of Republican funeral music. But Beethoven's music goes well beyond its prototypes; a quite separate and elaborate secondary theme follows, in addition to a middle section that for a few moments offers welcome relief from all the grandeur and solemnity.

Next comes a swift, exquisitely light-footed Scherzo with a central Trio that features declamatory (and precariously difficult) solo roles for the three horns. Then the finale begins with an outraged flurry in the strings, leading to a dead stop on a series of expectant dominant chords. What follows is puzzling: a fragmentary, sketchy bit in the strings that hardly qualifies as a theme or melody. Beethoven nevertheless offers a couple of leisurely variations on this mysterious thing. Finally, the real first theme enters, and we learn that the tune we have been listening to all this time was only its bass line. Now the music unfolds into an eloquent, energetic movement combining elements of theme-and-variation and rondo.

Viennese audiences first heard the *Eroica* at two concerts early in 1805; their reactions ran the gamut from admiration to disdain. At some point during the first public performance of this—the world's longest—symphony, a member of the audience reportedly stood up and shouted, "I'll give another kreutzer [a Viennese coin] if the thing would only stop." One critic wrote that the symphony "often loses itself in lawlessness," and found in it "too much that is glaring and bizarre," while another reported the opinion of a Beethoven friend that "this symphony is his singular masterpiece, the true style for music of the highest order."

So, who was the hero Beethoven celebrated in the *Eroica*? As he began the work, it was unquestionably Napoleon, but events in Bonaparte's campaigns unfolded in quick succession while Beethoven was writing his symphony. And in May 1804, when the work neared completion, Napoleon declared himself Emperor of France. Beethoven's student Ferdinand Ries recalled the composer's reaction:

> In this symphony Beethoven had Buonaparte in mind, but as he was when he was first consul. Beethoven esteemed him greatly at the time and likened him to the greatest Roman consuls. I as well as several of his more intimate friends saw a copy of the score lying on his table, with the word "Buonaparte" at the extreme top of the title page, and at the extreme bottom, "Luigi van Beethoven," but not another word . . .
>
> I was the first to bring him the news that Buonaparte had proclaimed himself emperor, whereupon he flew into a rage and shouted: "So he too is nothing more than an ordinary man. Now he also will trample all human rights underfoot, and only to pander to his own ambition; he will place himself above everyone else and become a tyrant!"
>
> Beethoven went to the table, took hold of the title page at the top, ripped it all the way through, and flung it on the

floor. The first page was written anew and only then did the symphony receive the title *Sinfonia eroica*.

Whatever credence we wish to grant this famous story, it surely appears that Beethoven changed the title of the symphony at some point before it was published in 1806 under the title *Sinfonia eroica*. A surviving title-page in the composer's hand, evidently intended for his Viennese publisher and dated August 1804, reads: "Sinfonia grande/intitolata Bonaparte." The words "intitolata Bonaparte" have been so violently erased as to tear a hole in the paper. But it may be that the composer's motives in this matter were less idealistic than Ries remembered. For Napoleon's army marched into Vienna in the autumn of 1805, scattering the nobility and occupying their palaces—including that of Beethoven's faithful patron Prince Lobkowitz, to whom he dedicated the symphony. It would hardly be politic to pay a public tribute at this moment to the invader. Still, in a letter from about the same time to a publisher friend in Leipzig, the composer confided that "the symphony is really entitled Bonaparte."

Like many Europeans of a generally liberal bent, Beethoven had difficulty making up his mind: was Napoleon a self-made hero dispensing democratic principles born of the French Revolution around Europe, or was he simply a ruthless conqueror and dictator? And even if, as Ries claimed, Beethoven intended the symphony as a tribute to Napoleon, there was something distinctly abstract about the project: it featured an elaborate funeral march for a hero not yet dead.

Fidelio

Beethoven felt an affinity for all things French. He spent his youth in Bonn among enthusiasts of the French Enlightenment and (initially, at least) of the Revolution. As a young man, he long entertained a vague thought of moving to Paris—the dedication of his "Kreutzer" Sonata of 1803 to this foremost musician of that city, Rodolphe Kreutzer, was one sign of his admiration for the French—and in a letter of early 1804 to his friend Joseph Sonnleithner he wrote of his "unshakable" determination to make the move.

His next big project, the only opera he ever finished, *Fidelio*, involved another French connection. Republican France provided the source for its libretto: *Léonore, ou l'amour conjugal*, with a text by J. N. Bouilly and music by Pierre Gaveau, had been performed in Paris in 1798. This was a "rescue opera," reflecting the current French appetite for terrifying tales of dungeons, executions, and hairbreadth escapes that recalled the *frissons* of life during the Revolution. In Beethoven's opera (translated into German by Joseph Sonnleithner), the hero Florestan, a political prisoner, languishes in a dungeon; on orders from the wicked prison commander, Don Pizzaro, the jailor Rocco is about to put him to death. But Florestan's wife, Leonore, masquerading as a male attendant named "Fidelio," interposes herself at the last second, pistol in hand, to stop the killing. And at this crucial moment the benevolent minister of state, Don Fernando (announced by a fine trumpet fanfare), intervenes to set all things aright.

There is a single dramatic event, the rescue. And there are three central characters, two good and one evil. Other persons and events are peripheral: a pair of ingénue-servants (Jaquino and Marzellina), the self-serving jailor Rocco, the imagined day-to-day life at the prison, and the inevitable amatory confusion owing to the ambiguity of Leonore's gender.

Beethoven's contract with the Theater an der Wien for *Vestas Feuer* ended at the beginning of 1805; he moved out of his rooms there, ironically just at the moment when he began working in earnest on his new opera, slated for performance on the same stage. From early 1805 until late autumn of that year, he devoted himself almost exclusively to *Fidelio* (or *Leonore*, the name Beethoven preferred, but could not urge on its producers).

Beethoven explained to Sonnleithner, the librettist, that the only sections of the book he needed immediately were the "poetical parts," that is, the texts for arias and ensemble numbers. For German operas, like French comic operas and American musicals, advanced the action by spoken dialogue, as opposed to the recitative of Italian opera. (We note this distinction in Mozart's *Die Zauberflöte—The Magic Flute*—with its spoken text, as opposed to the Italian-language *Don Giovanni*, where the conversations are set in recitative.)

Fidelio straddles the line between the serious and the comic. A high-minded rescue and a celebration of the triumph of good over evil occupy its dramatic center. On the other hand, the subsidiary characters—Jacquino, Marzelline, and Rocco—offer the familiar situations of comic opera: activities and concerns of everyday life, complaints about status, servants who mix flirtation with work and mislead their employers. Accordingly, Beethoven created soaring, idealistic music for one faction and simpler, plain-spun tunes for the other. The first big section of the opera (two acts, later compressed into one) mainly shows the subsidiary characters as they go about their duties; Beethoven reserved the main events—the introduction of the prisoner Florestan, his rescue and its celebration—for the final act.

In the first act, after two numbers of good-natured bantering among the jail workers, Leonore joins them in a splendid quartet, "Mir ist so wunderbar" ("For me it is so fine") that instantly changes the tone of the proceedings. The four singers enter singly in a leisurely fugal beginning that evolves into a good bit of coloratura singing by Leonore, in which Marzelline, remarkably, joins her. In the following number, Rocco instantly reverts to a more home-spun tone as he contemplates a possible marriage between Marzelline (his daughter) and the supposed young man Fidelio: "Hat man nicht auch Gold beineben" ("If you don't also have money"). In the first act finale, prisoners supply the expected chorus as they rejoice upon being released into the open prison yard: "O welche Lust" ("Oh what joy"), an ensemble in the resonant close harmonies of the German men's chorus ("Männerchor") which was then gaining popularity wherever that language was spoken.

The principal action begins with the second (and final) act: we see Florestan, languishing in a barely-lit dungeon, chained to a rock; the orchestra plays ominous music that leads to his "accompanied recitative," "Gott! Welch Dunkel hier!" ("God, what darkness here!"). In accompanied recitative, generally reserved for dramatic highpoints, the orchestra plays bits of agitated material between the singer's phrases, serving to whip up maximum tension and dread. This prepares us for Florestan's great soaring aria, "In des Lebens Frühlingstagen" ("In the Springtime of Life"), where he reflects on his past life (one of rectitude) and his willingness now, if he must, to endure this suffering. The music climbs again and again to the very top of the tenor's range, the drama heightened by adroit orchestral accompaniment. Yet another section follows: Florestan, in a state of agitated delirium, sees visions of his angel, Leonora, coming to comfort him—after which he sinks exhausted to the cold floor.

Rocco and Leonore then make their way down to the dungeon, followed by the villain Pizzaro, intent upon the hero's death. Florestan joins them in a quartet that presents the dramatic climax of the opera: Pizarro moves to stab Florestan, whereupon Leonore produces her pistol and justice is restored. The main characters and the prisoners (all apparently unjustly incarcerated) move up to the sun-lit courtyard, where the townspeople join them for the celebratory finale. Ensembles of soloists alternate with the massed chorus in a scene of ecstasy that foreshadows the finale of the Ninth Symphony from nearly two decades later.

The premiere of *Fidelio* was scheduled for the middle of October 1805, but Beethoven didn't put the finishing touches on the work until some weeks later, and this delay turned out to be crucial. That month, Napoleon's armies were moving toward Vienna. On October 30, French forces under General Bernadotte captured Salzburg and proceeded down the Danube toward Vienna. The aristocracy of the city, most of Beethoven's potential audience, saw what was coming and began packing up and moving out. The Empress left on November 9. On November 15, Napoleon himself took up residence in Schönbrunn Palace just outside of the city walls, as other French notables moved into the various splendid vacated residences around the city; one General Hulin made himself comfortable in the palace of Beethoven's attentive patron, Prince Lobkowitz.

The following week, on November 20, *Fidelio, oder die eheliche Liebe* ("Fidelio, or Married Love") opened at the Theater an der Wien. A few of Beethoven's friends were in the audience, and a few French soldiers wandered in and out. According to a local paper, no one attended the performance the following evening, and after a third performance the evening after that, the show closed. Beethoven's concentrated work of at least a year seemed lost.

Reviews of the opera also disappointed: according to one critic, "The melodies as well as the general character ... lack that happy, clear, magical expression of emotion that grips us so irresistibly in the works of Mozart and Cherubini." Even Beethoven's friends expressed reservations, particularly about the too-long and rather inert first act. The next month several of them, including the composer's younger brother Caspar Carl (now living in Vienna), met with some of the performing musicians at the home of Beethoven's faithful patron Prince Lichnowsky to persuade him to make changes. According to one witness, after some six hours of struggle they overcame the composer's furious objections; he made extensive revisions, eliminating three numbers from the first act and combining it with the second.

The revised version was performed several times the following spring with much greater success—until the composer, feeling cheated in his share of ticket sales, shut the production down. *Fidelio* then disappeared until 1814, when a third, highly successful incarnation put the work on the road to a permanent place in the European repertory.

The *Fidelio* project of 1805-06 also made its contribution to Beethoven's trove of instrumental music, the area of his work to which he owed most of his growing fame: three new overtures, Leonore nos. 1, 2, and 3. Leonore No. 1 Beethoven discarded before the premiere in 1805; Nos. 2 and 3 accompanied the performances of 1805 and 1806, respectively. (He wrote yet another overture for the 1814 revival, now called *Fidelio*.) Best known of all these is the splendid *Leonore* No 3, often performed independently on concert programs.

During this period of great productivity, there were also developments in Beethoven's personal life. As early as 1799, he had met members of the aristocratic Hungarian Brunsvik family who frequently visited Vienna. Beethoven became friendly with various family members and gave piano lessons to two daughters, Therese and Josephine. Josephine, aged 20, soon married a wealthy Viennese businessman named Von Deym but continued her association with the composer. After von Deym's death in 1804, Beethoven fell passionately in love with her—as some 14 of his letters attest. In one, from the fall of 1807, he told her that he had called on her twice during her stay in Vienna, "but I was not so fortunate as to see you—that hurt me deeply." In a final letter to her, Beethoven wrote, "Please deliver the sonata to your brother, dear Josephine—I thank you for wishing still to appear as if I were not altogether banished from your memory." The pattern is a familiar one: Beethoven grew enamored of a much younger piano student whose age and higher social class make their official union impossible. In 1810, Josephine duly married a proper aristocrat, one Baron Christoph Stackelberg.

Although Beethoven's absorption with *Fidelio* in 1804-05 limited his energy for other big projects, the sketchbook that records his struggles with the opera also features his work on one of his best-known works for piano, the *Appassionata* Sonata, Op. 57, completed in 1805. But when *Fidelio* was finished in the fall of that year, the floodgates of productivity swung wide, bringing into being one remarkable work after another, including some of the most admired music of his "middle period."

4. Scaling the Heights, 1806-1809

Works discussed in the present chapter:

Fourth Piano Concerto, Op. 58

Fifth Symphony, Op. 67

Sixth Symphony ("The Pastoral"), Op. 68

One foreign city where Beethoven's instrumental music was greatly valued during this period was London. There, Muzio Clementi, the distinguished pianist-composer turned music publisher, was instrumental in making Beethoven's works known. Passing through Vienna in the spring of 1807, he set about acquiring exclusive English publication rights for a good number of the composer's recent works. In correspondence with his partner back in London, Clementi described the encounters between the two musicians thus:

> By a little management and without committing myself, I have at last made a compleat conquest of that *haughty beauty*, Beethoven, who first began at public places to grin and coquet with me, which I of course took care not to discourage ... meeting him by chance one day in the street—"where do you lodge?" says he; "I have not seen you this *long* while!"—upon which I gave him my address. Two days after I found on my table his card brought by himself, from the maid's description of his lovely form ... Three days after that he calls again, and finds me at home ... "are you engaged with any publisher in London"?—"No" says he. "Suppose, then, that you prefer me?"—"With all my heart."
>
> "Done."

The contract Beethoven drew up with Clementi provided English rights to all of his most recent instrumental music: the Fourth Piano Concerto, three String Quartets (Op. 59), the Fourth Symphony, his overture to Heinrich von Collin's play *Coriolan*, and the Violin Concerto (including the composer's own piano transcription of the solo part). But because at this time Napoleon's "continental system" forbade the passage of goods between England and the continent, Clementi's letter to his partner specifies, "To-day sets off a courier for London through Russia, and he will bring over to you two or three of the mentioned articles." In a letter to Franz von Brunsvik (Josephine's brother), Beethoven exulted: "I just want to tell you that I came to a really satisfactory arrangement with Clementi—I shall receive 200 Pds. Sterling—and besides I am privileged to sell the same works in Germany and France." Beethoven also wrote to publishers in Bonn and Paris, offering the same works, with the stipulation that they were to appear only after a certain date.

Here we see the composer beginning to work out a plan for "simultaneous publication," Beethoven's novel way of increasing his share of the proceeds from the sale of his works. It was standard practice among music publishers to pay composers not royalties, but a one-time fee for their work. But in the absence of international copyright laws, publishers could simply reprint music from abroad; or companies in different countries could collude in sharing the music they had acquired—thus also splitting the composer's fee. In a letter of 1804, Clementi himself offered to "go halves" with Breitkopf & Härtel in acquiring Beethoven's music for publication. But in time, Beethoven accumulated enough clout with music publishers in several countries to insist on a single date of publication—and collect his fee from each.

Among the compositions Beethoven sold to Clementi were two concertos, one for piano (the Fourth) and the other for violin (his only one for that instrument). The concerto was typically a vehicle for composers who were also virtuoso performers (many leading composers from Beethoven's century were also virtuoso keyboard players: Bach, Mozart, Clementi, and Johann Nepomuk Hummel;

Handel and Haydn were not solo performers). Mozart and Beethoven typically played their piano concertos at public concerts, some consisting entirely of their own works. Neither was in any hurry to publish his concertos, thus allowing for further performances and on-the-spot revisions. The most extreme example of this tinkering in Beethoven's oeuvre is the "Second" Concerto (which actually existed in more than one version before the "First"). He played and revised this piece repeatedly from about 1790 to 1800.

Essential to the concerto is its alternation of a solo (or sometimes a small group) with the larger ensemble, thus evoking a very old and widespread sort of human expression: a discourse of the individual and the group, or of leader and followers. This was a familiar practice in, for example, Christian worship going back to the early Middle Ages: responsorial psalm-singing in which a soloist sang verses interspersed with choral responds; it also shows up in some of the finest moments in the later 19th-century comic operas of W. S. Gilbert and Arthur Sullivan.

It is standard practice in concertos from the time of Mozart and Beethoven for the large group to go first (the players and what they play are called a "tutti"). Just as in the instrumental introductions to big operatic arias, the opening orchestral tutti presents most of the musical substance of the movement. Next comes a "solo" section where the soloist leads the way, presenting riffs and embellishments on this material—usually plus a new theme or two—with the orchestra accompanying and responding. For the rest of the movement, solo and (abbreviated) tutti sections alternate until, in an interruption of the final tutti, the soloist enters with a cadenza: a (supposedly) on-the-spot improvisation on some of the themes we have just heard leading to a decisive cadence (or ending), after which the orchestra finishes off the movement in short order. Here it is in graphic form:

T1   S1   T2 S2   T3 S3   T4 (S cad.) T5

But in his Fourth Concerto, Beethoven has the piano go first—with a brief, poignant sounding of the opening theme, a statement that ends not in closure, but with a question mark. The orchestra then takes up where the piano had left off, proceeding with its rather leisurely exposition of the main thematic matter of the movement. That opening "question" in various forms dominates this section, sometimes rising to heights of great emphasis and passion. There is only one contrasting bit of music: a quiet, tense tune, stated three times in different keys, passed from the violins to the woodwinds, whose snapping rhythms suggests perhaps a military march in the distance. But this lasts only a moment; the orchestra quickly sweeps it away, ending this introductory section with the question still hanging in the air.

Now the piano soloist takes over with an improvisatory-sounding riff on that main theme—as if to suggest a couple of ways the orchestra's question might be approached. Soon the piano leads the way in commenting on and embroidering those two now-familiar main tunes—while adding a third one that comprises characteristics of both. In the second big solo, the piano part grows more abstract, serving up scintillating, agile ornamentation of the themes at hand, usually in a very high register, as the orchestra follows along obediently, often clarifying the thematic connections within the piano's flights of fancy. Throughout this movement, Beethoven positively luxuriates in the upper reaches of the piano keyboard's newly expanded range, offering his listeners a fresh perspective on piano sound.

But the most startlingly original movement of this remarkable concerto is the second one. This striking interlude, less than five minutes long, offers us a vividly etched dialogue between piano and strings. The conversation begins in dead earnest discord, but in the end, achieves at least an uneasy resolution. The strings start off in stentorian tones, with agitated jagged staccato octaves: a proclamation that would seem to brook no opposition. The piano's answer sounds less like opposition than near-irrelevance: lost in its own musings, it traces a subdued (in fact *pianissimo*) songful downward melodic path, heavy with resignation. This opening evokes a dramatic (almost operatic) scene in which implacable demand—or prohibition or censure—is met with a certain grave and muted reflection of only tenuous pertinence.

The orchestra and piano continue this exchange with an almost ritual symmetry, the orchestra insistent, the piano meditative and subdued. But presently the piano begins to crowd out its imperious adversary, cutting it short with ever more insistent plaints until it breaks out, at last, into a flowing lyrical statement. This grows increasingly insistent (and loud) as the strings remain silent. Finally, things calm down, the strings enter, quiet and cowed; the piano and its adversary come to a muted, peaceful conclusion.

What are we to make of all this? Such musical rhetoric seems intimately bound up with situation, character, speech. And there are also clear elements of human drama: a protagonist and antagonist whose positions change over time from implacable opposition to something like reconciliation, maybe even agreement. Beginning in the mid-19th century, a succession of writers (one was E. M. Forster) concluded that Beethoven must have modeled his movement on some literary or dramatic source. The most commonly mentioned candidate was the scene in Christoph Willibald Gluck's *Orfeo ed Euridice* (first performed in Vienna in 1762), in which Orpheus pleads with the Shades in Hades for the release of his beloved Euridice. As Orpheus's entreaties grow ever more fervent, the Shades gradually relent from their pitiless refusal and allow him to lead Euridice to the world above (though, we recall, in this legend as recorded by Ovid, things didn't turn out so well).

We do not know whether Beethoven had any such specific model in mind. We do know that in his world listeners routinely recognized a repertory of passions or affects common to dramatic situations and rhetorical or musical utterances. Entertaining such associations now should probably depend on the individual listener's inclinations: if such links clarify or enrich the musical experience, they perform a service.

Growing productivity and income

The Fourth Piano Concerto, in 1806, was a product of a period of astounding productivity for Beethoven; in that year alone he also composed the three String Quartets, Op. 59; the Violin Concerto; the Fourth Symphony; and the *Leonore* Overture No. 3; as well as a number of piano pieces (one was Thirty-Two Variations on an original theme). At this time, the composer continued to benefit hugely from the support of his highly-placed patrons. Prince Joseph Franz Maximilian Lobkowitz, himself an excellent violinist and cellist, kept a private orchestra in his palatial home (at 1 Lobkowitz Platz), where in the spring of 1806 Beethoven gave two concerts of his own works, including the first four symphonies, a piano concerto (likely the fourth), and the Overture to von Collin's play, *Coriolan*. Events such as these gave the composer matchless opportunities to try out his new music before public performance or publication.

Relations with another patron, Prince Karl (skipping five other forenames) Lichnowsky, turned sour. In about 1801, Lichnowsky had presented the composer with a quartet of valuable Italian string instruments (probably in connection with the composition of his first set of String Quartets, Op. 18); about this time he also granted Beethoven an annuity of 600 florins (roughly $25,000) per year "until he could find a suitable position," continuing these payments until at least 1806.

In the late summer and fall of that year, the composer spent some weeks at Lichnowsky's summer home in Grätz (Prussia). His spirits were apparently low after the semi-failure of *Fidelio*—and his usual volatility correspondingly high. According to his friend, the musician and author Ignaz Seyfried, one evening, pestered by the guests, French officers, who wished to hear him play, he grew angry and refused to do what he denounced as menial labor. A threat of arrest, surely made in jest, he took seriously, and it resulted in his walking by night to the nearest city, Troppau, whence he hurried as on the wings of the wind by extra post to Vienna.

War, according to the quaint custom of the time, did not prevent members of the upper crust of opposing sides from spending sociable evenings together. But (according to another of Beethoven's friends), the incident at Grätz occurred shortly after the battle at nearby Jena in which Napoleon's forces resoundingly defeated the Prussians—a battle that greatly distressed Beethoven and prompted his famous retort, "It's a pity I do not understand the art of war as well as I do the art of music; [otherwise] I would defeat him." In any event, Beethoven's refusal to play and his abrupt departure that evening evidently created a rift with Lichnowsky that was never quite repaired.

Lichnowsky's expectation that Beethoven would one day "find a suitable position" could have meant only one thing: that he would enter the employ of some highly-placed patron's musical establishment, and pursue his career as Haydn had done for many years under the aegis of the Esterhazys. But such a course was the last thing Beethoven—with his rather advanced notions of the dignity of the artist—would have entertained. He was splendidly skilled, in any case, at exacting benefits from patrons without becoming their servant. And he was, moreover, in the vanguard of artists in the new century who increasingly directed their efforts toward a new "patron:" that emerging social construct taking shape in European cities, one with its own powers and preferences, the public.

The principal arenas where musicians presented their wares to the public were the opera theaters that often doubled as concert halls. Vienna had three big theaters suitable for opera or large-scale concerts: the two court theaters (the Burgtheater and the Kärntnertor Theater), and the Theater an der Wien just outside the city, the site of Beethoven's concert of 1802 and of the premiere of *Fidelio*. All operated under the ultimate control of the Imperial government. Late in 1807, a shake-up of the management of the three theaters put their governance into the hands of a committee that included some of Beethoven's ardent admirers, notably Princes Lobkowitz and Esterhazy. Beethoven saw an opening and made a bold and novel proposal to the new directors: that each year he would provide "at least one" grand opera, and some smaller offerings—according to the wishes of the directors—for which he would receive a yearly salary, a share in the profits of the opera, and the guaranteed use of a theater for a yearly concert for his own benefit. Lurking in this proposal was a repeated implication that in the absence of such an agreement he might well move elsewhere.

The management of the theaters soon changed again, and Beethoven's proposal came to nothing. But in the following year, 1808, another, altogether unanticipated proposal for a radical career change arose—this one beckoning the composer back toward the old patronage system. It came about this way: as Napoleon marched through Europe, conquering one region after another, he set up new governmental authorities, often putting his relatives in charge. One such region, in central Germany, became the "Kingdom of Westphalia," centered in Kassel. Its new king, anointed in 1807, was Jérôme Bonaparte, Napoleon's 22-year-old brother, who reportedly devoted his energies mostly to a famously dissipated lifestyle. But the following year, he moved to add a bit of class to his newly created court by offering Beethoven the position of Kapellmeister (the person ultimately responsible for all the music at court). But as this court had no musical establishment, Beethoven would be required only to play occasionally for the young king, and to organize a concert now and then.

It is hard to know whether the composer ever seriously contemplated moving, or simply used the Kassel offer as a bargaining chip. In January of 1809, he wrote to his publisher in Leipzig, Breitkopf & Härtel, insisting, with his chronic dose of paranoia:

> At last owing to intrigues and cabals and meannesses of all kinds I am compelled to leave my German fatherland which is still in its way unique. For I have accepted an offer from His Royal Majesty of Westphalia to settle there as Kapellmeister at a yearly salary of 600 gold ducats.

But several of the composer's highly placed admirers moved quickly to keep him in Vienna. At the suggestion of the Countess Erdödy,

Beethoven drew up a list of his requirements for staying: an annuity equal to the Kassel offer (600 gold ducats—the equivalent of roughly $90,000—plus travel expenses) to be paid "until he voluntarily renounces it" with no specific duties attached; and the guarantee of one concert date a year at the Theater an der Wien.

Three of Beethoven's admirers stepped up and agreed to share the cost of this remarkable project: Prince Lobkowitz; Beethoven's new student the young Archduke Rudolph (son of Leopold II, the previous Emperor); and the young military commander Prince Ferdinand Kinsky, who had no known previous contact with the composer. By the terms of this extraordinary arrangement, ratified in a contract of March 1809, Beethoven was to become a truly independent agent, relieved of financial concerns, and free to practice his art as he saw fit. But, as we shall see, this blessed state of freedom was not to last.

The question of the move/annuity unfolded during a period of splendid productivity for Beethoven that saw the birth of, among other works, the iconic Fifth Symphony and the Sixth Symphony (the *Pastoral*). Eager to present his new music to a Viennese audience, he engaged in frustrating negotiations with the management of the Theater an der Wien for a concert date. Hoping to move the management in his favor, Beethoven agreed to conduct one of the theater's charity concerts in November 1808. Preparations for that concert seem to have been something of a disaster: at a rehearsal, according to one report, Beethoven "first swept the candles off the piano, and then knocked down a choir-boy deputed to hold them by his too energetic motions." Members of the orchestra grew so upset that they refused to continue the rehearsal under his direction. The record does not reveal how the concert went. But, in any case, Beethoven achieved his goal and was granted use of the theater for his concert the following month.

Making the most of this opportunity, he loaded the program with the two new Symphonies, the Fourth Piano Concerto, a series of vocal pieces, and, as a grand finale, the newly-composed *Choral Fantasy*, a hybrid of oratorio and concerto with solo piano, chorus, and orchestra. A visiting composer-author from northern Germany, Johann Friedrich Reichardt, reported,

> I accepted the kind offer of Prince Lobkowitz to let me sit in his box with hearty thanks. There we continued, in the bitterest cold, from half past six to half past ten, and we experienced the truth that one can easily have too much of a good thing—and still more of a loud . . . The box was in the first balcony near the stage, so that the orchestra, with Beethoven in the middle conducting it was below us and near at hand; thus many a failure in the performance vexed our patience in the highest degree.

Apparently, things went most wrong in the barely-completed *Choral Fantasy* (a musician reported that at the rehearsal the voice parts were "as usual, still wet"). A widely-read musical journal described what happened:

> The wind instruments varied the theme Beethoven had previously played on the pianoforte. The oboes' turn came. But the clarinets make a mistake in the count and enter at once. A curious mixture of tones results. Beethoven jumps up, tries to silence the clarinets, but does not succeed until he has called out quite loudly and rather ill-temperedly: "Stop, stop! That will never do! Again—again!"

If we could have attended Beethoven's concert, we would probably have found the general level of performance shocking—and not only in the *Choral Fantasy*. Preparations for this massive program were distinctly hasty. In Vienna in those days, professional orchestral musicians routinely played concerts after only one rehearsal. Such fleeting preparation may have been minimally effective for music in a familiar style. But Beethoven's two big symphonies alone, first heard that December evening in a cold hall, placed entirely new technical and interpretive demands on the players. And it is probably safe to say that in his entire lifetime Beethoven never heard his orchestral music performed with the exactness and attention to detail we now consider routine.

The Fifth and Sixth Symphonies

After completing his Fourth Symphony in 1806, Beethoven made a conscious decision to compose symphonies in contrasting pairs. The first pair could hardly have been more different: the Fifth with its heaven-storming crescendos and air of victorious affirmation, and the Sixth with its quiet musing on the joys of nature.

The Fifth begins, of course, with more of a rhythm than a tune: three dots and a dash. During World War II, both sides used this rhythm as a symbol for victory, for it spelled out "V" in Morse Code—a connection Beethoven knew nothing about, as Morse Code came into being some 25 years after the symphony. This rhythm keeps showing up elsewhere in the work. The third movement, an elaborate scherzo and trio that never really ends, sliding mysteriously into the triumphant finale, features that rhythm in its main melody. And there it is again in the finale, as a building block of a subsidiary theme, and then, very pointedly, just before the jubilant recapitulation, in a mysterious, explicit interlude that revisits the first movement.

For the exultant finale of this symphony, Beethoven reinforced his orchestra with some new instruments: three trombones (instruments with both celebratory and otherworldly associations) and a piccolo. With all the instruments playing at maximum volume, the music thrusts upward with an air of both striving and exultation. Three other distinct themes follow; some begin in a more subdued, lyrical vein, but all devolve into something similarly exclamatory.

Many of Beethoven's listeners would have found the manner of this finale rather familiar: it recalls the spirit and sounds of mass public celebrations (*fêtes*) the French staged during the revolution and early Napoleonic days. The *fêtes* were intended to whip up patriotic enthusiasm in the masses; a principal figure in the French Revolution, Maximilien Robespierre, called them "an essential part of public education." The government eventually settled on seven such events a year, staged at various locations around the country. The sort of music heard there was reflected in the many patriotic songs that were printed and widely distributed; best known of these is the present-day French national anthem, *La Marseillaise*, its words and music composed in 1792 by an army captain, Rouget de Lisle. Its vigorous upward melodic thrusts and general tone of exultation are faithfully mirrored in the finale of Beethoven's Fifth.

What are we to make of Beethoven's embrace of this sort of French music, a style rife with political implications? When the French revolution exploded in 1789, Beethoven was an impressionable 18-year-old living in Bonn, surrounded by adults of a liberal persuasion who wholeheartedly approved of the revolution's newly-minted ideals of equality and freedom. And although Napoleon disappointed Beethoven later—and there is good reason to think that disappointment was always mixed with a certain admiration—the original motivating goals of the French Revolution never stopped inspiring him, and echoes of its music were a permanent part of the composer's style.

The other symphony heard at Beethoven's 1808 concert, the Sixth, or *Pastoral*, inhabits a different world. The music of the Fifth strives for declarative resolutions, for triumphantly reached goals, while the Sixth seems content in its own skin, happy to be where it is, soaking up the pleasures of a gentle landscape.

Beethoven equipped the five movements of this symphony with descriptive titles. The first is called "Awakening of cheerful feelings on arrival in the country." Over a bass suggestive of a drone—an effect routinely associated with rustic music—the violins play a bucolic melody that hesitates briefly, then carries on with serene repetitions of simple shapes, as if there is no particular goal in sight, only the enjoyment of the present. Later in the movement, when the music finally rises to fortissimo, it suggests something more like simple enthusiasm than triumph. The second movement ends with the most explicit programmatic touch anywhere in Beethoven's oeuvre: imitations, specified in the score, of the calls of the nightingale (flute), the quail (oboe), and the cuckoo (clarinet). Such musical imitations of natural sounds—often called "tone-painting"—were much discussed, and, often, derided in Beethoven's day. We can detect his own uneasiness with the subject in the note he added to the concert program of 1808: "More the expression of feeling than painting."

Next comes a movement called "scene by the brook" with appropriate murmuring of a gentle current, followed by "merry gathering of country folk" where Beethoven gives us his impression of peasant holiday music (static harmony and lots of drones). This happy scene is then interrupted by a "Thunderstorm." It starts with an ominous shift of key, gathers strength quickly, and (with the aid of newly introduced trumpet and tympani) explodes in a furious mass of sound with obsessive short scales in the bass and falling figures above—presently joined by violin imitations of lightning bolts (going up, curiously, rather than down). Peace is at last restored in the finale, "Shepherd's song: happy and grateful feelings after the storm," where Beethoven rings endless changes, often supremely artful, on a quiet, simple tune.

The Pastoral Symphony is, among Beethoven's big instrumental pieces, virtually unique in its prevailing peace and serenity. There is little sign here—not even in the storm section—of that familiar Beethovenian striving after big goals or the celebration of their attainment that follows. About the closest competitor in overall serenity of tone is probably the Piano Sonata in D major, Op. 28, of 1801—a piece that is, without the composer's blessing, often called the "Pastoral Sonata."

In the spring of 1809, having just finished a series of major big pieces, the heart of his "middle-period" work, Beethoven set about concluding the terms for the "annuity contract" that would, at last, put his finances in order. While as late as January 1809 he had complained to his Leipzig publisher, Breitkopf & Härtel, about the vexations of life in Vienna—"the intrigues and cabals and contemptible actions of all kinds" that were prompting him to leave—the contract now maintained that "Beethoven has so great a predilection for life in this city, so much gratitude for the many proofs of good will he has received here, and so much patriotism for his second fatherland that he will never cease to count himself among the Austrian artists."

Looking for love

Having achieved, as he thought, a degree of stability in his life, Beethoven turned to his recurring thoughts on another subject. In a jocular letter to his friend Ignaz von Gleichenstein, who was about to leave on a trip to Germany, he wrote:

> Now you can help me hunt for a wife. If you find a beautiful one in Freiburg, who yields a sigh to my harmonies . . . make connections with her in advance. But she must be beautiful, for I cannot love that which is not beautiful—else I should love myself.

Upon his return to Vienna in January 1810, Gleichenstein, intentionally or not, complied with Beethoven's request by introducing him to the family of Jacob Malfatti, a prosperous banker and businessman who had two daughters, Therese and Anna. Beethoven much enjoyed the Malfatti's company and became a frequent visitor. In a grateful letter to Gleichenstein he wrote, "I am so happy when I am with them. I feel somehow that the wounds which wicked people have inflicted on my soul could be cured by the Malfattis."

The 40-old composer was particularly attracted to Therese, age 18, and even took some measures to improve his personal appearance. He asked Gleichenstein—"since I understand so little about these things"—to buy him "linen or Bengal for shirts and at least a half-dozen neckties." He apparently proposed to Therese and wrote to his old friend in Bonn, Franz Gerhard Wegeler, asking him to obtain his baptismal certificate and send it to him as soon as possible. But it was all to no avail. In what was to become a consistent pattern, Beethoven had taken an interest in an unattainable woman; Therese was thought to be above his social class, and, moreover, inappropriately young. A letter from Gleichenstein (now lost) seems to have informed Beethoven that he was no longer welcome at the Malfatti house except when he took part in music there. Devastated, he replied, "Your news has plunged me from the heights of the most sublime ecstasy down into the depths... Therefore only in my own heart can I again find something to lean upon... For you, poor B[eethoven], no happiness can come from outside."

There is an intriguing footnote to this sad story. Beethoven had clearly exchanged music and books with Therese, and in early 1810 he composed some pieces mainly for her, among them the songs "Wonne der Wehmut" ("The bliss of melancholy") and "Sehnsucht" ("Longing"). One other such piece is a Bagatelle for piano composed in the spring of 1810. The autograph manuscript, now lost, bore an inscription in the composer's hand which a 19th-century scholar first read as "Für Elise" ("For Elise"); under that name, this little piece has become perhaps Beethoven's most widely known composition, played ceaselessly by piano pupils throughout the Western world. Beethoven scholars had wondered for decades who was this mysterious "Elise," as there was no known woman of that name among his acquaintances. But the composer's handwriting was notoriously hard to read, and a reputable researcher confirmed in 1925–before the manuscript disappeared–that the dedication reads not "Für Elise," but "Für Therese." This tribute to his lost love was lost to history through a misreading.

5. Difficult Times, 1809-11

Works discussed in the present chapter:

Fifth Piano Concerto ("The Emperor"), Op. 73

Overture to "Egmont," Op. 84

Piano Sonata ("Farewell"), Op. 81a

The little drama of Beethoven's infatuation with Therese played out against a scene of crisis and despair in Vienna. For in May of 1809, Napoleon's very large and efficient army marched once more into the city. The Austrian military hastily assembled an armed force for its defense. This army cut the bridges to the city and concentrated its forces north of the Danube, where, after a terrible battle at the town of Wagram, they were utterly defeated and sued for peace. The nobility, not at all sanguine about the outcome, had once again—as it had during Napoleon's invasion of 1805—packed their bags and retreated to safer places. During an intense bombardment of Vienna, Beethoven, according to his student and biographer Ferdinand Ries, hid in the cellar of his brother's home in the interior of the city, where he covered his head with pillows to shield his sensitive ears from the explosions. In July, he wrote to his Leipzig publishers, Breitkopf & Härtel:

> Let me tell you that since the fourth of May I have produced very little coherent work, at most a fragment here and there. The whole course of events has in my case affected both body and soul. I cannot yet give myself up to the enjoyment of the country life which is so indispensable to me—The existence I had built up only a short time before rests on shaky foundations—and even during this last short period I have not yet seen the promises made to me completely fulfilled—So far I have not received a farthing from Prince Kin-

sky . . . What a destructive, disorderly life I see and hear around me, nothing but drums, cannons, and human misery in every form.

Beethoven's anxiety about the singular financial arrangements he had made with his benefactors would prove to be well-founded; his annuity was to become a casualty of the Austrian defeat. A drastic devaluation of the Austrian currency effected by the *Finanz-Patent* of 1811 vastly reduced the worth of the sum to which he was legally entitled. In November 1811, moreover, Prince Kinsky died after a fall from his horse, and Prince Lobkowitz, long a lavish supporter of music in Vienna, went bankrupt and stopped his payments to Beethoven (who then sued unsuccessfully for their reinstatement).

During this period, Beethoven continued to move restlessly from one dwelling to another in the city (during his 35 years in Vienna, he lived in at least 20 different places). In the winter of 1808-09, he occupied rooms in the residence of his admirer, the Countess Anna Maria Erdödy. Visiting from Germany, the musician-author Johann Friedrich Reichardt remarked upon watching the Countess listen with rapt attention to Beethoven's music: "Fortunate the artist who can count upon such listeners!" But, as so often happened in the composer's relationships, a misunderstanding arose (this one about a servant of Beethoven's, whose salary she had secretly been supplementing) and Beethoven promptly moved out. And, as also often happened, he later regretted his behavior:

My dear Countess,

I have erred, that is true—forgive me. It was assuredly not intentional malice on my part if I have hurt you—only since last evening have I known what the truth is, and I am very sorry how I behaved.

Beethoven's new apartment was in the Walfischgasse, very close to the city wall—and to Napoleon's cannons that had prompted his retreat to his brother Carl's place during the attack of May of 1809.

During the following year he moved twice more, the second time into the fourth floor of a house owned by the Baron Pasqualati, where he had lived for a time some six years earlier, and where now, finally, he was to remain for almost four years.

During the earlier part of this chaotic episode in his life—in fact, just as Napoleon was advancing on and invading Vienna—Beethoven was busy composing the piano concerto widely known as "The Emperor." This name is a later invention and, to say the least, historically dubious. If its composer had entertained any such association, it would be hard to guess even which emperor he might have had in mind: Napoleon, who was presently making his life a misery, or maybe the hapless Emperor Franz of Austria, no match for Napoleon and now about to surrender once more to the French?

The truth, of course, is that this concerto has no legitimate connection with any emperor. And though its themes and rhythms at every turn suggest the "heroic," even something like military pageantry, we can hardly imagine that Beethoven, oppressed by all the "drums, cannons, and human misery" about him, could have intended this music as a celebration of any military hero or anybody's victory in war. The symbolism here, as in most music of substance, is far subtler—at once richer and more diffuse than the mere property of being "about" an emperor, a battle, military heroes, or battles in general. Any invocation of such things in this music we should think of as distinctly metaphorical: thoughts of the military, that constant presence in Beethoven's world, likely reminded him (and now us) of a generalized human struggle, and its heroic gestures pointed to a certain nobility of character required to master the situation.

Beethoven's Fourth Concerto, we recall, had quite exceptionally started out with the solo piano playing the main theme, thus getting the central musical argument underway. The Fifth Concerto begins with three brilliant cadenza-like flourishes from the soloist, each set in motion by a stentorian chord from the orchestra. Rather than launching the main argument of the movement, this introduction seems to intimate something like character: the protagonist as brilliant, masterful, starting a purposeful motion toward the real beginning of the piece—and yet showing a certain reserve and forethought, turning *espressivo* (expressive) as each of the stations along the way is approached. We are left with the impression of a decisive protagonist with an imaginative flair tempered by a certain bent toward reflection: an impression that will color our hearing of the entire movement.

The main body of the movement is built upon just two themes. The first is an assertive, swashbuckling march with distinctive snapping upbeats (a precision change in direction?). The other theme, always in a high register, is pianissimo, but tense with understated pent-up energy. A common element between them is an underlying regular stride. Each in its own way intimates the idea of a military march—the first extroverted with brass blaring, the second evoking martial motions only at a distance, as in imagination or memory. (Later it will shed its reserve, change from minor to major, and become a march pure and simple.) Out of these two musical ideas and their derivatives, Beethoven constructed a movement of memorable grandeur, with a wealth of original keyboard sound that at every turn implies character and drama.

Commenting on the following slow movement, the composer's younger contemporary and one-time student Carl Czerny reported, "When Beethoven wrote this *Adagio*, the religious songs of devout pilgrims were present in his mind, and the performance of this movement must therefore perfectly express the holy calm and devotion which such an image naturally excites." Descriptive words such as "hymn-like" and "meditative" indeed seem on the mark for this music. The opening melody is played by muted low-lying violins to an almost magical calming effect. The piano responds with a passage of limpid, unhurried, descending figures above long-held tones in the bass that recall the first melody. We hear differing versions of that tune in its entirety twice more, until a ruminative, unhurried figuration in the piano stretches out to meet the finale.

There is one catch: the second movement is in a key (B major) very distant from that of the outer two movements (E♭ major).

Beethoven evidently thought of this second movement as an extended introduction to the third, and wished to connect the two. But, while it had always been the practice in the music of this period to move to a new key gradually and artfully, Beethoven will have none of it: the strings and bassoons simply step directly down to where the music needs to be. There the piano, still moving in the slow-motion of the movement at hand, mysteriously limns out the shape of the rondo theme to come. Finally, after a tantalizing pause on the upbeat, that theme comes on in a rush, galumphing upward in irregular, good-natured bounds. Then in the downward reply, there is clarification: this is a hunting theme, its rhythm recalling, say, the first movement of Mozart's "Hunt" Quartet (K. 458) or the finale of Haydn's Symphony No. 73, "La Chasse."

It is just that the beginning of Beethoven's theme seems distorted by an excess of energy—behaving for the moment more like a large puppy than a reliable steed. From this entertaining theme and two subsidiary ideas, he fashioned a memorable rondo finale where the outspoken military implications of the first movement are replaced by more peaceful motions—at least for the humans involved—of the hunt.

Beethoven had composed all his previous four piano concertos mainly for his own performances, and had officiated at the keyboard as both soloist and conductor for each of their premieres. This was not the case with the Fifth Concerto. By 1809, he had largely given up playing in public, partly because of the increasing demands on his time of composition and publication of his works, and also, surely, because of the continued decline of his hearing (early that year, he scribbled in a sketchbook, "Cotton in my ears at the piano frees my hearing from the unpleasant buzzing"). Thus, the Fifth Concerto got its first public hearing in November 1811, in Vienna, with one Friedrich Schneider at the keyboard.

Difficult times in Vienna

During their occupation of the city, the French imposed draconian penalties on its inhabitants. From owners of houses, for example, they exacted from one quarter to one half of the yearly rent the owners collected. Prices rose exponentially and the necessities of life, including food, became scarce. The suffering, of course, was borne almost exclusively by those on the lower rungs of the social ladder; the nobility and other people of means remained discretely elsewhere, out of harm's way. Beethoven was one of those left behind in occupied Vienna, and in 1809 he felt prevented even from making his annual summer-time escape to a country retreat. A young admirer reported seeing the composer shake his fist at a passing French officer and exclaim, "If I, as a general, knew as much about strategy as I the composer know about counterpoint, I'd give you something to do!"

But one occupying French officer, a certain Baron de Trémont, who was a music lover and ardent admirer of Beethoven, recalled, "I admired his genius and knew his works by heart . . . I made up my mind that in case the army should take Vienna I must not neglect the opportunity to see Beethoven." Despite the awkwardness of the situation, Beethoven received the Frenchman several times and evidently even improvised for him at the piano. Trémont continued:

> I believe that to these improvisations of Beethoven's I owe my most vivid musical impressions. Unless one has heard him improvise well and quite at ease one can but imperfectly appreciate the vast scope of his genius. Swayed wholly by the impulse of the moment, he sometimes said to me, after striking a few chords: "Nothing comes into my head; let's put it off till–" then we would talk philosophy, religion, politics, and especially of Shakespeare, his idol . . .
>
> His mind was much occupied with the greatness of Napoleon, and he often spoke to me about it. Through all his

resentment I could see that he admired his rise from such obscure beginnings; this appealed to his democratic sentiments.

We should not be particularly surprised that Beethoven talked about philosophy, religion, and politics with this French aristocrat (though it is hard to guess which language they used; Beethoven's French was rudimentary, and the French tended to despise German). Although his formal schooling had ended by his 11th year, Beethoven consistently made serious efforts at self-education, reading widely in the classics, as defined in German-speaking parts of Europe. In a letter of 1809 to Breitkopf & Härtel, he named as his favorite writers Homer, Goethe, Schiller, and Ossian. (This last, a shadowy third-century figure in Celtic literature, was much in vogue at the time—though, as it turned out, his "translator," the 18th-century Scott James MacPherson, actually manufactured most of his "writings." Beethoven undoubtedly read Ossian in the recent German translations of J. G. Herder.)

The current enthusiasm in Europe for the literature and customs of the Near East, particularly Persia, also attracted the composer's attention. Herder and the contemporary Austrian Orientalist and historian Joseph von Hammer had published translations of Persian poetry that Beethoven read eagerly. And going yet further afield, he was attracted by elements of Hindu belief; here is an excerpt from a long passage he copied into one of his manuscripts:

> Brahma; his spirit is unwrapped in himself. He, the mighty one, is present in every part of space—his omniscience is in spirit by himself and the conception of him comprehends every other one; of all comprehensive attributes that of omniscience is the greatest . . . O God, thou art the true, eternal, blessed, immutable light of all times and all spaces . . . thou alone art the truly blessed one; thou, the essence of all laws, the image of all wisdom, present throughout the universe.

Having grown up in the intellectual environment of the high Enlightenment, with its marked suspicion of religious belief, Beethoven persistently aspired to some form of understanding beyond the bounds of this material world. Though just what he believed always seemed rather inchoate, he was apparently drawn to a species of "natural religion" akin to Deism; here is a famous exclamation he wrote into one of his sketchbooks: "The moral law within us and the starry heavens above us. Kant!!!"

For a composer with only one opera to his credit (*Leonore/Fidelio*), Beethoven invested a good deal of thought and planning into this most prestigious of musical genres. During 1809-10, he consulted intently with a local poet and dramatist, Heinrich von Collin—author of the play *Coriolan* for which he had composed an overture in 1807—about possible librettos. One for which he made some sketches was Collin's versified version of *Macbeth*. But with the French in charge, the official court theater (Burgtheater) offered little but French fare, thus squeezing German productions into the remaining theaters, particularly the Kärntnerthor, thus severely limiting any local composer's prospect of mounting a new opera.

But in the fall of 1809, the manager of the court theaters, Joseph Hartl, presented Beethoven with a related opportunity: to compose an overture and incidental music for a new production of Goethe's play, *Egmont*. This drama presents the noble Flemish Count Egmont, who bravely endures imprisonment by the despotic Spanish conqueror, the Duke of Alba, and dies a hero's death in defense of justice and national liberty—just the sort of thing that would appeal to Beethoven when his own adopted country was under foreign occupation. He composed an overture and 10 further numbers including entre-acts, songs, and one melodrama (a genre reserved for points of high tension that featured spoken text with interspersed instrumental exclamations). After its premiere in 1810, Goethe's play had largely been forgotten; Beethoven's overture is the only part of the entire enterprise that has had much of an afterlife.

A slow introduction to the piece starts with a stern, tense statement in the strings with snapping upbeats suggesting a situation of high gravity in a context of military precision; a wandering, distracted-sounding reply in the strings sounds like a nervous, uncertain reaction to that situation. The main body of the movement remains consistently dark and foreboding—a second theme repeats that unrelenting first military rhythm—until the very end, where all is magically transformed: the entire orchestra joins in ecstatic major-key celebratory music that ends the piece on a note of triumph. This music gives us a foretaste of the "Victory Symphony," the last of the 10 numbers Beethoven wrote for the play. Goethe's drama ends with Egmont's death, but his very martyrdom is cast as a victory over oppression.

During this period of French occupation Beethoven, like most residents of Vienna, struggled with the ordinary necessities of life. He was long accustomed to taking his meals out, often at a local restaurant, "The Swan." But later in 1809, dissatisfied with the current state of restaurant food, he laid plans to begin dining at home. To that end, he set about hiring two servants—the sort of task that, mainly due to his deafness, he always entrusted to one of the friends available to do his bidding, in this case, Nikolaus Zmeskall:

> Today Herzog, who wishes to become my servant, will come to see you—you may engage him for 30fl. with his wife—wood, light, a small amount of livery. I must have someone to cook for me, for as long as the present wretched food continues I shall remain ill.—Today I am dining at home, because of the better wine. If you will order what you want, I shall be glad to have you come to eat with me—you will get the wine gratis and indeed a better one than that at the beastly Swan.

Beethoven did engage the Herzogs but, as often happened in this irascible and impractical man's practical affairs, things soon went awry. He explained to Zmeskall:

> I do not want to see that woman again, and although she is perhaps better than he, I want to hear as little about her as

about him . . . You will hear more from me in person concerning how much she has recently lied to you . . . Besides I found her several times with her husband down below at the watchmaker's in my house; she even wanted to go out from there with him when I needed her. Therefore, I let him come back, since I had to keep her for my lodgings. If I hadn't taken him back I would have been cheated all the more—so the matter ends; they are both wretched people.

Thus, Beethoven continued to be a familiar figure in the neighborhood restaurants.

As early as 1803, Beethoven had attracted the attention of George Thomson of Edinburgh, a music publisher who specialized in printing national airs of the British Isles in arrangements by Europe's foremost composers (one was Haydn). He attempted to enlist Beethoven in his project and for some time the two haggled (in French) about Thomson's already handsome offers of payment. Finally, in the fall of 1809, Thomson sent the composer 43 Welsh and Irish songs, requesting that he provide them "as soon as possible" with ritornellos and accompaniments for piano or pedal harp with other accompanying string instruments. Beethoven again asked for substantially more money than Thomson was offering as "this work is of a kind that gives a composer but little pleasure," adding, "Next time please send me the words of the songs along with them, as they are very necessary in order to get the correct expression."

Over the next dozen or so years, Beethoven arranged a very large body of songs for Thomson—tunes from the British Isles, but also folksongs in various continental languages. As he seemed to imply in 1809, Beethoven at first apparently undertook this sort of work simply for the money involved. But the contemporary high estimation of folksong as the genuine expression of a "people" also struck a responsive note in him, and some of his settings—which Thomson occasionally complained were too difficult to perform—are worthy of this great composer.

The Romantic Beethoven

The first decade of the new century saw the stirrings of a powerful new romantic movement among German writers. Centered in Jena and Berlin, it exerted a decisive effect on views of contemporary music; Beethoven's music was squarely in the center of this movement. Foremost among these writers was the extravagantly imaginative novelist (also a composer, theater director, and jurist) E. T. A. Hoffmann. Hoffmann had a special taste for the humorous, mysterious and supernatural, as in his collection *Lebensansichten des Katers Murr, nebst fragmentarischer Biographie des Kapellmeisters Johannes Kreisler* (Life Perspectives of the Tom Cat Murr, Plus a Fragmentary Biography of the Music Director Johannes Kreisler). He found these qualities in abundance in music, particularly Beethoven's.

In 1810, Hoffmann published the first of a series of long reviews of Beethoven's Fifth Symphony, the *Egmont* music, and several other compositions, in the musical journal, *Allgemeine musikalische Zeitung* of Leipzig. Here is a sample of what he said:

> When we speak of music as an independent art, should we not always restrict our meaning to instrumental music, which, scorning every aid, every admixture of another art (the art of poetry), gives pure expression to music's specific nature, recognizable in this form alone? It is the most romantic of all the arts—one might say, the only genuinely romantic one—for its sole subject is the infinite. The lyre of Orpheus opened the portals of Orcus—music discloses to man an unknown realm, a world that has nothing in common with the external sensuous world that surrounds him, a world in which he leaves behind him all definite feelings to surrender himself to an inexpressible longing.

This supreme power of music, he tells us, came about only gradually in the procession from Haydn to Mozart, and then to its culmination in Beethoven:

> Haydn grasps romantically what is human in human life; he is more commensurable... Mozart calls rather for the superhuman, the wondrous element that abides in inner being. Beethoven sets in motion the lever of fear, of awe, of horror, of suffering, and wakens just that infinite longing which is the essence of romanticism.

In views of art in the 18th-century Enlightenment, music had always been something of a puzzle: it wasn't obviously *about* anything. Plays, poems, and paintings, on the other hand, had identifiable subjects that music seemed to lack. If a composition included a verbal text, as in a song or opera, its music was generally seen as a reinforcement or embellishment of its meaning. But suppose there was no text, as in a sonata or symphony? Eighteenth-century German music theorists wrote out elaborate tables of short snatches of music with suggestions as to the sort of verbal text that they could appropriately accompany: listeners were invited to supply their own interpretation. But lack of a clear subject or meaning in instrumental music was always seen as a deficiency.

Now, several romantics, led by Hoffmann, saw music—particularly music unsullied with a text—as highest among the arts. For the subject or meaning of music was much more exalted than the text of a song or the dialogue of an opera: the value of art in general (and of music in particular) lay in its connection to a transcendental order, to a supernatural level apprehendable in no other way. Eight years after Hoffmann's Fifth Symphony review, in *The World as Will and Representation*, the philosopher Arthur Schopenhauer named that ultimate level of truth and being to which the romantics aspired "The Will." While all the other arts afforded some glimpses of it through their subject matter, he said, music, without a subject, was the "direct representation of The Will."

Self-designated romantics of Beethoven's time, from about 1810, clearly counted Beethoven as one of their number. This estimation of his place in the history of the arts contradicts the usual present-day designation of historical periods in European music, wherein

Beethoven joins Haydn and Mozart as representative of a "classical period." The romantic era, that story goes, starts with Beethoven's younger contemporary, Franz Schubert, and lasts for the rest of the nineteenth century. But this formulation ignores much of Beethoven's later compositional career and contemporaneous views of the matter.

Meeting new people

Another prominent poet of the romantic persuasion with whom Beethoven had contact was Clemens Brentano. The Brentano family, of Italian origin, had established itself in the business world of Frankfurt in the 17th century and in time gained great wealth and influence on various fronts. Clemens Brentano, widely known for his novels and plays, joined with Achim von Arnim to produce, between 1805 and 1808, that seminal document of German Romanticism, an expansive collection of folk poems named *Des Knaben Wunderhorn* (The Boy's Magic Horn). Brentano greatly esteemed Beethoven, met with him several times in Vienna, and offered him poems for composition—none of which the composer ever used.

Brentano's sister Elisabeth (known as Bettina), married to Arnim, was a prominent figure in literary circles; Goethe was among her friends. She met Beethoven in Vienna in 1810 and instantly became his passionate admirer—some later commentators have speculated about a romantic attachment. Many years later, Bettina published a detailed account of her interaction with Beethoven, in which the composer spoke in a suspiciously exalted literary language ("all this Beethoven said to me"). Here is a small sample:

> When I open my eyes I must sigh, for what I see is contrary to my religion, and I must despise the world which does not know that music is a higher revelation than all wisdom and philosophy, the wine which inspires one to new generative

processes, and I am the Bacchus who presses out this glorious wine for mankind and makes them spiritually drunk.

Bettina also published some letters she claimed the composer wrote to her, but most of these are now judged a fabrication. One genuine letter of Beethoven's to Bettina (from 1811) survives: here the composer indulges in some affectionate banter, and wishes her well in her impending marriage to Arnim: "May all the happiness and blessings which marriage bestows upon a wedded couple be yours and your husband's in full measure."

One more Brentano in Beethoven's circle became so by marriage: Antonie von Birkenstock, daughter of a noted Viennese art collector, was married to the much older Franz Brentano, head of the family's business and banking interests in Frankfurt. While in Vienna, she and her family became close to Beethoven. He played in concerts at their home; when she was indisposed and unable to leave her room, she later reported, Beethoven would call, seat himself at the piano in the anteroom, improvise for her, and leave without speaking to anyone. In the next chapter, we will hear more about Antonie Brentano.

In 1810-11, Beethoven continued to toy with the idea of a new opera. One possibility he seriously entertained was a French drama on a theme from ancient history, *Les Ruines de Babylone*. He obtained a German translation and conscripted a friend, the playwright and theater manager Georg Treitschke, to refashion the play into a libretto; but as always seemed to happen when Beethoven contemplated a new opera, he let the project drop. But three years later, Treitschke was to be instrumental in producing a new version of the composer's only opera, *Fidelio*.

One likely reason that Beethoven did not move forward with the new opera is that in 1811 he was extraordinarily busy supervising the publication of his most recent music. Early in the year, with his Leipzig publisher alone, Breitkopf & Härtel, he had a whole series of major compositions in the works: a piano concerto (the "Emperor"), the Choral Fantasy for chorus, piano, and orchestra, the oratorio *Christus am Ölberge* ("Christ on the Mount of Olives"), a piano sonata, and two sets of German songs. Beethoven read proofs of his music compulsively, and regaled his publisher with complaints about their shortcomings: "Errors–errors–you yourselves are one large error . . . It appears as if the musical tribunal at L[eipzig] is unable to produce a single decent proof reader."

Another matter worrying Beethoven (never free from a touch of paranoia) was the danger that other publishers would get hold of his music and issue it without authorization (and without payment to the composer). As his own handwritten manuscripts were mainly illegible except to the practiced eye, a copyist was needed to make a readable score. To keep his copyists from spiriting away his work and selling it, Beethoven tried to have them work in his lodgings, under his watchful eye. It didn't seem to work; that spring, he wrote to his faithful patron Archduke Rudolph:

> Since despite all my exertions I could find no copyist who would work at my house, I am sending you my manuscript. You would be most kind just to send it to Schlemmer [Beethoven's principal copyist] for a capable copyist who must, however, copy the trio only in your palace, as otherwise one is never safe from *theft*.

Another possible factor in Beethoven's reluctance to launch into so massive an undertaking as a new opera was his health. Always precarious, in the spring of 1811 it became especially troublesome, with (among other things) severe and unrelenting headaches. As the strictures of the French occupation of the city were no longer in force—the Treaty of Schönbrunn had rendered the French and Austrians putative allies—in July, on the recommendation of his physician, Beethoven traveled to the spa town of Teplitz (now Bad Teplice in the Czech Republic), known for its healing waters. He arranged for a young friend, Franz Oliva, to meet him there and serve as a copyist and general assistant; arriving in Teplitz in August 1811, he set about availing himself of the waters and continued reading proof for his impending publications.

Spas across Europe were favorite summertime meeting places

for reasonably well-off people from many walks of life. In Teplitz, Beethoven was among a medley of remarkable people, most of whom he sought to avoid. But he seemed to gravitate toward certain literary figures. One was the young German poet and biographer Varnhagen von Ense, whose memoirs recall interactions with the composer:

> His deafness made him shy, and his peculiarities, which had become more marked through separation from other people, limited the little circulating he did . . . yet in Teplitz he sat down at the piano and played his newest, still unknown things or indulged in free fantasy . . . I found the man in him even more appealing than the artist. And when a close friendship between Oliva and me developed soon thereafter, I was also together with Beethoven and gained a still closer relationship with him through the prospect, to which he clung eagerly, that I could supply or revise texts for him for dramatic composition.

Another service von Ense supplied was to urge Prince Ferdinand Kinsky, one of the three guarantors of Beethoven's annuity agreement (who was also present in Teplitz), to pay the composer what he owed. Kinsky immediately agreed, but shortly thereafter, unfortunately, fell from his horse and died, closing off that part of Beethoven's income.

An older poet Beethoven met that summer in Teplitz was Christophe August Tiedge of Dresden, known mainly as the author of *Urania*, a long, philosophical poem in the tradition of Schiller; later Beethoven wrote to him, "Every day I scold myself for not having made your acquaintance at Teplitz sooner. It is dreadful to come to know goodness so briefly and then to lose it once more . . . Let us embrace like men who have cause to love and honor one another." And traveling in Tiedge's party was a rising star from Berlin, the 24-year-old opera singer Amalie Sebald. She and Beethoven seem to have gotten well acquainted; in the letter to Tiedge he sent her "a very ardent kiss when no one sees us." While some later commentators have posited a serious romantic relationship between the two, a series of short, rather prosaic notes Beethoven wrote to her the following summer argues against it.

In September 1811, Beethoven finally left Teplitz, making rather a wide detour to Troppau (presently Opava in the Czech Republic) to visit his patron Prince Karl Lichnowsky at his country estate, and to supervise the performance of his Mass in C in the town. He declined an invitation from even farther east for the dedication of a new theater in Budapest, where some of his music was to be performed. He was at home by early October.

Return to Vienna

Waiting for him was a shipment of his newly printed scores from Breitkopf & Härtel, who, in addition to music of all sorts, also published the leading journal about music in Germany, the *Allgemeine musikalische Zeitung*. Thus, the company dealt with Beethoven, rather awkwardly, in two very different ways: as a producer of his music and as a critic thereof. A long letter to B&H from this time registers the composer's annoyance at the response to his music in the journal:

> I am sorry that I ever said a word about those miserable reviews. Who can mind what such reviewers say when he sees how they elevate the most wretched scribblers, and how they treat most insultingly works of art to which they cannot at once apply their standard as a shoemaker does his last, as indeed they must do because of their incompetence.

In the same letter, Beethoven is also dryly critical of the edition he had just received of his Sonata, Op. 81a, titled *Lebewohl*, or "Farewell." (The score calls it "Les Adieux," which, he claimed, is much less personal than "Lebewohl.") Perhaps the most programmatic of all Beethoven's instrumental compositions, this sonata records his purported feelings about the Archduke Rudolph's leaving the city during the French occupation of Vienna in 1809-1810. Beethoven supplied exacting superscripts: first movement, "The Farewell. Vienna, 4 May 1809 on the departure of his Imperial Majesty the Esteemed Archduke Rudolph"; second movement, "Absence"; third movement, "Return." The descending musical motif of the opening movement imitates the signal of the post horn, that small brass instrument that mailmen throughout Europe and England used to announce the arrival and departure of the post coach. (In composed music, it usually meant departure). The second movement registers abject dejection through poignant dissonance and a certain aimlessness of direction, while in the third, marked "vivacissimamente," the joy in its reckless racing motion is irresistible.

All this personal feeling for the 23-year-old nobleman, a member of the Imperial family, should be taken with a grain of salt. It is clear from the composer's correspondence with friends that the Archduke's demands on him (such as several lessons a week) were frequently burdensome; his periodic absences were clearly something of a relief. But—exceptionally for Beethoven—the formal relationship of patron and artist prevailed here mainly, it seems, because the composer's financial wellbeing depended upon it.

6. Distraction and Coping: 1812-15

Works discussed in the present chapter:

Seventh Symphony, Op. 92

Eighth Symphony, Op. 93

"Wellington's Victory: The Battle at Vittoria," Op. 91

Piano Sonata, Op. 90

In June of 1812, Beethoven and all of Europe anxiously awaited reports of Napoleon's latest venture—his ill-fated invasion of Russia. The French army, greatly swelled with forced recruits from vassal countries, numbered about 450,000 men as they marched across the vast area from the Neman River (in present-day Lithuania) toward Moscow. The Tsar's opposing army, no match for Napoleon's troops, simply retreated, adopting a scorched-earth policy that left the French with little but burned and abandoned villages and destroyed fields. Fewer than a quarter of Napoleon's men survived long enough to enter Moscow in September, only to find that the city was also deserted and in flames. Tsar Alexander, 300 miles away in St. Petersburg, refused to negotiate with the invaders. Napoleon and the remnants of his army had no choice but to begin the long trek home through winter snows, finally re-crossing the Neman in December with a contingent of only 30,000 starving men—a tiny fraction of the army that had ventured forth a few months earlier.

Meanwhile, that summer, Beethoven returned to the spa town of Teplitz, where he had sojourned the previous year. There, he joined an exalted circle of dignitaries awaiting the outcome of Napoleon's Russia campaign. Among them were the Austrian Emperor Franz I and his then Empress, Maria Theresa, together with assorted kings, dukes, and counts from eastern Europe, all of whom hoped fervently for a French defeat. (It may have been a bit awkward that Marie Louise, 19, the Emperor's daughter, was also there: she had become Napoleon's wife in a marriage of convenience the previous year.) While the assembled nobility rejoiced in Teplitz, Napoleon, as-yet undeterred, hurried back to Paris to assemble a new army for the pursuit of further campaigns in Germany.

Beethoven surely joined in celebrating Napoleon's defeat, but that summer he had other things on his mind. Shortly after his arrival in Teplitz, he wrote the first installment of a long, three-part, rather disjointed letter that has been generating speculation and debate among Beethoven scholars for a century and a half. This is an agonizingly intense love letter addressed to an unnamed "immortal beloved," (*unsterbliche Geliebte*), whom he expected soon to join him. Since it was found in his papers after his death, he likely never sent it. Here are some excerpts:

> My angel, my all, my very self, only a few words today—Oh God, look at the beauties of nature and quiet your soul over that which must be—love demands everything, and quite rightly, so it is for me with you, for you with me—But you forget so easily that I must live for me and for you. If we were fully united, you would feel this painful necessity as little as I would . . .
>
> We will surely see each other soon, and today I cannot share with you my thoughts of the last few days about my life—were our hearts truly together I would feel no hindrance to unburdening my breast completely. Oh, there are moments when I find language of no use.
>
> Even lying in bed my thoughts rush to you, my immortal beloved, now and then happily, or again sorrowfully, waiting for fate, whether it will hear us—I can live either entirely with you or not at all. I have decided to wander far away until I can fly into your arms and declare myself entirely at rest

with you, my soul embraced in you, and transported to the realm of the spirits.

For much of his adult life, Beethoven habitually engaged in relationships with women, some more earnest than others. In almost every case, the object of his affections was well out of his reach, whether because of social standing, youth, or both. The "immortal beloved," however, presented an attraction of another order: his attestations of love for her were profoundly serious—and evidently reciprocated.

Beginning shortly after the composer's death, writers about Beethoven have advanced five or six different women as likely candidates for the "immortal beloved" distinction. Then in 1972, the American Beethoven scholar Maynard Solomon convincingly identified the intended recipient of the letter as Antonie Brentano (though this has hardly put an end to the controversy).

Antonie, as mentioned in the previous chapter, was the daughter of Johann von Birkenstock, a Viennese diplomat and wealthy art collector. After her mother's early death, her father placed Antonie in a cloister where she remained for seven years until her arranged marriage, at the age of 18, to Franz Brentano, the wealthy Frankfurt banker 15 years her senior. By the age of 26, she had four surviving children and had effectively taken charge of the expansive Brentano family. Ill and desperately homesick for Vienna, she returned there with her children in 1809 to care for her dying father, and stayed for three further years to settle his affairs. During this time, it seems, she met Beethoven.

Franz Brentano, Antonie's husband, also spent a good bit of time in Vienna during this period, and, on the surface at least, Beethoven became and remained a friend to both of them, even after the couple returned to Frankfurt, and for years thereafter. He dedicated minor compositions to their children; they lent him money when he needed it, and in 1819 Antonie commissioned the fashionable painter Joseph Stieler to execute a portrait in oil of their friend.

We do not know whether in the summer of 1812 Beethoven succeeded in meeting the "immortal beloved" in Teplitz. But she was surely not there when he complained to his friend Varnhagen von Ense, "There is not much to be said for Teplitz; few people and among the few nothing extraordinary, wherefore I live alone! alone! alone! alone!" But later in the summer, he met at least one person there who should count as extraordinary: the magisterial German author, then at the height of his fame, Johann Wolfgang von Goethe. In a letter to a friend, Goethe captured something of Beethoven's sour mood of the time:

> I made Beethoven's acquaintance in Teplitz. His talent amazed me; unfortunately he is an utterly untamed personality, who is not altogether in the wrong in holding the world to be detestable, but surely does not make it any the more enjoyable either for himself or others by his attitude. He is easily excused, on the other hand, and much to be pitied, as his hearing is leaving him, which, perhaps, mars the musical part of his nature less than the social.

By September, though persistently bedridden with digestive ills, Beethoven seemed more like his old self and resumed some of his customary social habits. In affectionate exchanges with Amalie von Sebald, a singer from Berlin he had first met in Teplitz the previous summer, he wrote: "I am already better, dear A. If you think it proper to come to me alone, you could give me great pleasure; but if you think it improper, you know how I honor the liberty of all people."

Early in October, Beethoven finally departed Teplitz but took a slight detour southward to visit his younger brother Johann, now a prosperous pharmacist in Linz, some distance up the Danube from Vienna. Beethoven's intentions in making this visit were not merely fraternal. Living with Johann in his large house was a young woman, Therese van Obermayer, together with her illegitimate daughter from a previous relationship. Beethoven went to great lengths to break up this arrangement, appealing to both church and civil authorities to have the woman removed. After a court order directed the police to send her back to her native Vienna by a certain date, Johann quickly married her, thus thwarting the efforts of his older brother and presenting him with a new and not particularly welcome sister-in-law. This episode showed a couple of things: the composer's continuing feelings of protectiveness—sometimes veering toward the domineering—in respect to his younger brothers (Johann was now in his mid-30s), and a certain streak of prudishness that seemed to attach particularly to them.

Productive summer

Just before his summer travels in 1812, Beethoven finished his marvelous Seventh Symphony. This is a spacious, hugely energetic composition, dominated by dance rhythms that at points, particularly in the finale, play out with bacchanalian energy. But the second movement, *Allegretto*, is of a wholly different order: its sober, measured rhythm in dactyls and spondees, with a stationary melody on top, suggests a solemn procession akin to a funeral march (in essential ways it recalls the funereal slow movement of Beethoven's Sonata Op. 26).

This movement made a huge impression on Beethoven's audiences. A reviewer for the prestigious *Allgemeine musikalische Zeitung* in Leipzig wrote,

> The second movement, since its first performance in Vienna a favorite of all connoisseurs and amateurs, speaks inwardly even to those who have no training in music; through its naïveté and a certain secret magic it proves irresistible—and its repetition is demanded at every performance.

A somewhat less reverent London critic complained, "The Allegretto is like the single agreeable member of an unruly family, whom we seemingly cannot invite without having the whole lot of them."

Just as Beethoven had composed the Fifth and Sixth Symphonies more or less in tandem, he also produced the Seventh and Eighth in quick succession. Having just finished the Seventh, he took working materials with him on his travels in the summer of 1812, making substantial progress on the Eighth in Teplitz, and finishing it during the ill-fated visit to his brother Johann in Linz.

The Eighth, which Beethoven once called a "smaller symphony," is indeed the shortest of all his works in this genre. And—as in the case of the Fifth and Sixth—it offers a vivid contrast with its immediate predecessor.

The Seventh exudes power and high drama; the Eighth responds with cleverness, good cheer, and a wistful backward glance toward the high-classical manner of the previous generation, especially the symphonies of Haydn.

The first movement, for which Beethoven used materials initially intended for a piano concerto, is an exuberant piece with the balanced phrasing Haydn had tried to teach him. Only in the finale does Beethoven generate something of the muscular drive audiences expected to get from him. But just as the second movement of the Seventh has always particularly beguiled Beethoven's audiences, so, too, the second movement of the Eighth, *Allegretto scherzando*, has gotten a lion's share of attention. Almost throughout this piece, the winds play quiet, evenly spaced, obsessively repeated staccato chords. Well after the composer's death, Beethoven's early biographer, Anton Schindler, published a canon for four voices on the opening theme of the *Allegretto scherzando*, claiming Beethoven had composed it as a model for that second movement. The text of the canon celebrates the musician/inventor Johann Nepomuk Mälzel (1772-1838) and his best-known mechanical device, the metronome, which is still widely used by musicians to set tempos. (Those repeated chords, purportedly imitating the metronome's clicks, are sung to the syllables "ta. . .ta. . . ta"). Unfortunately, this story is apparently another fabrication of the notably devious Schindler, who likely composed the canon himself; a couple of glaring infelicities in the piece signal that this is not Beethoven's work. If those repeated chords in the Eighth Symphony are an imitation of anything, it is probably a similar movement from Haydn's Symphony No. 91, "The Clock."

Financial and family woes

Back in Vienna in November, Beethoven had contact with two well-known musicians who had recently arrived in the city. One was the distinguished French violinist Pierre Rode, for whom Beethoven quickly revised the finale of his newly composed sonata for piano and violin, Op. 96; Rode performed the piece with Archduke Rudolph at a concert at the Lobkowitz Palace in December. The other new arrival was a German violinist and composer just now gaining mounting fame throughout Europe, Ludwig Spohr (1784-1859). After several attempts to call on Beethoven, Spohr met him by chance in a restaurant, as he recalled in his autobiography:

> I had, by this time, already given a concert, and twice performed my oratorio. The Vienna newspapers had favorably reported on them. Hence Beethoven knew of me when I introduced myself to him and greeted me in an extremely friendly manner. We sat down together at a table, and Beethoven became very chatty, which greatly surprised the table company, as he generally looked straight ahead, morose and curt of speech. It was a difficult task to make him understand, as one had to shout so loudly that it could be heard three rooms distant. Afterward, Beethoven came often to this eating house and visited me at my lodgings, and thus we came to know each other well. Beethoven was frequently somewhat blunt, not to say rude; but an honest eye gleamed from under those bushy eyebrows.

Spohr's memories of an apparently cheerful Beethoven seem to be a bit misleading. For as Beethoven resumed his life in Vienna, memories of the "immortal beloved" episode continued to torment him. At the end of 1812, he began keeping a diary in which he recorded, in a rather disjointed fashion, his private thoughts and feelings:

> Submission, deepest submission to your fate, only this can

> give you the sacrifices—for this matter of service . . . Oh, hard struggle . . . you must find everything that your most cherished wish can grant, yet you must bend it to your will . . . You must be a human being, not for yourself, but only for others: for you there is no longer any happiness except within yourself, in your art—O God! give me strength to conquer myself, nothing at all must fetter me to life. In this manner with A everything goes to ruin.

And a few months later:

> O terrible circumstances, which do not suppress my longing for domesticity, but prevent its realization. O God, God, look down upon the unhappy B., do not let it continue like this any longer.

Adding to the anxiety and distraction in Beethoven's life was the condition of his younger brother, Caspar Carl, who lived in Vienna with his wife and son Karl, age 7. Caspar Carl, like so many citizens of Vienna, occupied a very minor position within the Imperial government, and in his spare time acted as an informal secretary and business manager for his composer brother. Now he suffered from tuberculosis. In the spring of 1813, his condition deteriorating, he wrote the following legal petition:

Declaration

> Inasmuch as I am convinced of the frank and upright disposition of my brother Ludwig van Beethoven, I desire that after my death he undertake the guardianship of my son, Karl Beethoven, a minor. I therefore request the honorable court to appoint my brother mentioned to the guardianship after my death and beg my dear brother to accept the office and aid my son in word and deed in all cases.

In designating Beethoven as his son's guardian, this document took away parental rights from Caspar Carl's wife Johanna, who some thought unreliable, and who had served a short prison sentence for fraud the previous year.

As it happened, Caspar Carl survived this crisis and lived for another two years. But while his financial situation had always been precarious and partially dependent on his famous brother, the devaluation of Viennese currency in 1811 made his condition critical. Beethoven, ever the protective—and often imperious—older brother, arranged a loan from a music publisher, putting up his future compositions as collateral. But despite this show of generosity, Beethoven's relationship with Caspar Carl was never simple. In later years, the son, Karl, recalled an incident from about the same time in which Beethoven burst into his brother's house, shouting "You thief! Where are my notes?" A violent quarrel followed, and Johanna had trouble separating the two brothers. When the score in question was produced, Beethoven begged forgiveness. But Caspar Carl remained angry, declaring that he never wished to have that dragon in his house again.

The currency devaluation or *Finanz-Patent*, also drastically affected Beethoven himself: what would become of the annuity from his three benefactors? The law clearly indicated that its value would greatly decrease. But Beethoven launched a barrage of correspondence pleading for what he felt was rightfully his. One of his donors, Prince Kinsky, we will recall, had fallen from his horse and died. So, Beethoven addressed his request to the widowed princess Kinsky (to whom he had earlier dedicated nine songs and whom, in a recent letter, he had described as "one of the prettiest and plumpest women in Vienna), assuring her that the Prince had promised to make up the difference. They finally reached a compromise in 1815. Of the three benefactors, only his faithful pupil Archduke Rudolph ever completely fulfilled Beethoven's expectations.

War and peace

Meanwhile, war in Europe continued. Napoleon retreated from Russia at the end of 1812 with the few exhausted soldiers who had survived. But instead of giving in to defeat, he hurried to Paris to raise fresh troops and to collect payments for military operations from occupied vassal states. But in several sectors he met with growing resistance: a natural resentment of renewed financial burdens combined with a growing spirit of nationalism—partly inspired by ideals of popular sovereignty born in the French Revolution—fed a new desire to cast off the French yoke. During the course of 1813, Prussia and Austria joined Russia in a declaration of war on France. When Napoleon's newly recruited troops won battles at Dresden and elsewhere in Germany in the summer of 1813, Beethoven wrote a dispirited letter to his friend Franz Brunsvik in Budapest:

> If the billows of war roll nearer here, I will come to Hungary. Perhaps I shall in any event, since I must need care only for my miserable self; I shall no doubt fight my way through. Away, nobler, loftier plans—infinite are our strivings, the commonplace puts an end to all.

But at just about this time, the fighting in Spain took a new turn. At the battle of Vittoria, British, Portuguese, and Spanish troops under the command of the English General Wellington soundly defeated the French army led by Napoleon's older brother, Joseph Bonaparte. And just a bit later, in October, the allies dealt the Grande Armeé what appeared to be their final defeat. The Viennese were delirious with joy and patriotism. In this heady atmosphere, Beethoven, who had once composed a symphony (the *Eroica*) in honor of Napoleon, now offered the public a little something to celebrate his downfall. In collaboration with Mälzel he composed a "battle piece" (a very fashionable genre at the time) called "Wellington's Victory." It was originally intended for performance on an invention of Mälzel's, the "panharmonicon"—a kind of elaborate barrel organ that could simulate the sound of various wind instruments. Then, at Mälzel's urging, Beethoven rewrote the piece for full orchestra, elevating it to the status of a "symphony;" the two of them envisioned a tour of England where they hoped this music would reap money and fame. Perhaps predictably, however, they quarreled over rights to the music, and the plans for England evaporated. Still, this unlikely composition had a reinvigorating effect on Beethoven's career.

The "Battle Symphony" is—surely intentionally on Beethoven's part—something of a spoof: a mishmash of noisy battle music, patriotic songs such as *Rule Britannia*, and, finally, a parodic fugal rendition of *God Save the King*. It premiered at a concert in Vienna in December 1813, with Beethoven conducting. Many leading musicians of the city participated, some (in keeping with the light-heartedness of the event), playing unaccustomed instruments. The composer-pianists Ignaz Moscheles, Johann Nepomuk Hummel, and Giacomo Meyerbeer, for example, were in charge of the percussion battery, whose principal duty was to sound like cannons.

Louis Spohr, playing in the violin section, had every opportunity to observe Beethoven's style as a conductor; he remembered it this way:

> Beethoven had accustomed himself to indicate expression to the orchestra by all manner of singular bodily movements. So often as a *sforzando* [a strong accent] occurred, he tore his arms, previously crossed upon his breast, with great vehemence asunder. At *piano* he crouched lower and lower as he desired the degree of softness. If a *crescendo* then entered he gradually rose again and at the entrance of the *forte* jumped into the air. Sometimes, too, he unconsciously shouted to strengthen the *forte* . . . It was obvious that the poor man could no longer hear the *piano*.

The audience was enraptured; the program had to be repeated a few days later, and again the following month. For the Viennese public, always fickle and sometimes—as Beethoven and others complained—shallow in their judgment, the performance of the "Battle

Symphony" was the composer's finest hour. It was, however, the only composition of any size that he produced in 1813.

Fidelio sees the light of day again

Beethoven's huge popularity with Viennese audiences suddenly presented the possibility of reviving his only opera, *Fidelio*. The premiere of this work, nearly coinciding with Napoleon's first conquest of Vienna in 1805, had bitterly disappointed the composer. For this new production, in 1814, he made major revisions. The actor and theater manager Georg Friedrich Treitschke rewrote the libretto, condensing the first two acts into one and moving the final scene from the dungeon where Florestan was imprisoned to the sunlit courtyard above. One telling change refashioned Florestan's big aria that opens the second act: it was originally all despair and resignation, but in 1814 it ended with the prisoner's delirious vision of a hovering figure that resembled his beloved Leonore. Treitschke recalled,

> We composed one thing and another: at last, in his opinion, I hit the nail on the head. I wrote words which describe the last blazing up of life before its extinguishment:
>
> . . .
>
> In the rosy fragrance I see an angel
>
> Coming with comfort to my side.
>
> An angel, so like my beloved Leonore,
>
> Who leads me to freedom—in heavenly realms!
>
> What I am now relating will live forever in my memory. Beethoven came to me about seven o'clock in the evening . . . He asked me how matters stood with the aria? It was

just finished, I handed it to him. He read, ran up and down the room, muttered, growled, as was his habit instead of singing—and tore open the pianoforte. My wife had often vainly begged him to play; today he placed the text in front of him and began to improvise marvelously—music which no magic could hold fast. Out of it he seemed to conjure the motive of the aria. The hours went by, but Beethoven improvised on.

The new version of *Fidelio* premiered at the principal court theater in May 1814, with the composer conducting (the leader of the violins reportedly took matters in hand when the hard-of-hearing Beethoven lost the beat). As the opera now began differently from the first version, Beethoven determined that it needed a new overture. But he postponed work on this until the last minute, and failed to finish it in time for the first performance. So that evening's entertainment began with the irrelevant Overture to *Creatures of Prometheus*, Beethoven's ballet score from 1800 (the new overture was ready for the performance two days later). The audience repeatedly erupted in tumultuous applause; a local newspaper remarked that "Herr van B was stormily called out already after the first act and enthusiastically greeted." This heady evening led to a series of repeat performances of *Fidelio*, as Beethoven's stock in Vienna rose to ever new heights.

The sketchbook in which Beethoven worked out his revisions to *Fidelio* also introduces a new piano composition, the Sonata in E, Op. 90, which he finished in August 1814. He dedicated the work to Count Moritz Lichnowsky, brother of Beethoven's generous benefactor, Prince Karl Lichnowsky, and a fine pianist. This rather modest piece has two movements. The first movement, in E minor, feels improvisatory: textures change easily, and sometimes it seems to suggest, rather than state, its musical themes. Though its manner is mainly rather subdued, there are occasional bursts of high emphasis (or maybe exasperation). The second movement, in E major, is a superbly lyrical rondo in which the melodious, understated main theme (or ritornello) returns again and again to striking effect. These two movements allow us an early glimpse of Beethoven's late (or "third-period") style: there is a loosening of formal bonds here that allows for free shifts of texture and figuration and a new unhurried melodic lyricism.

In the real world, meanwhile, Napoleon's army never recovered from the disastrous defeat at Leipzig in the fall of 1813. He could do nothing but retreat into France amid desperate negotiations with the allies for peace under somewhat favorable terms. But long-simmering resentments at home toward Napoleon, who had often expressed contempt for "la vile populace," roiled to the surface. The French Legislature declared him deposed, invited Louis XVIII back to the throne, and put up scant resistance as the allied armies marched into France. Napoleon officially accepted his fate in April 1814, sailing into exile on the Mediterranean island of Elba—over which his remarkably generous opponents had granted him full sovereignty together with a substantial pension.

Early that fall, the crowned heads and top diplomats from all the European nations began arriving for the Congress of Vienna; their main goal was to put Europe back together—in a distinctly retrospective fashion—after 25 years of nearly continuous war. The atmosphere during this seven-month affair was marvelously festive; celebration and dancing, some said, quite overshadowed planning and negotiation. As the Congress gathered, Beethoven cut short his summer stay in Baden and hurried back to the city to participate in his own way. He quickly produced some appropriate celebratory music, including "Chorus to the Assembled Princes" (its text begins "Thou wise founders of happy states"), and a more substantial cantata, *The Glorious Moment*, which opens with the exclamation "Europe stands firm!"

In November, many of the assembled dignitaries attended a concert of Beethoven's works that included the Battle Symphony *Wellington's Victory* (the Duke of Wellington, being present), *The Glorious Moment*, and the Seventh Symphony. The city's leading newspaper reported,

At noon yesterday, Hr. Ludwig v. Beethoven gave all music lovers an ecstatic pleasure. In the K. K. Redoutensaal he gave performances of his beautiful musical representation of Wellington's battle at Vitoria, preceded by the symphony which had been composed as a companion-piece [sic! The Seventh Symphony was quite unrelated to *Wellington's Victory*].

The concert was repeated twice the following month. And the first opera the Congress participants heard was the revised *Fidelio*; by October it saw its 16th performance. The author of the poem *The Glorious Moment*, Alois Weissenbach of Salzburg, exclaimed in his journal, "Today I went to the Court Theater and was carried to heaven—the opera *Fidelio* by L. v. Beethoven was given."

From early adulthood on, Beethoven had expressed sympathy for the Enlightenment notions of social equality loudly proclaimed in the early part of the French Revolution. Thus we might be surprised, maybe disappointed, to hear him, in those ephemeral "occasional" pieces starting with the Battle Symphony, joining in fawning adoration of Europe's newly reenergized nobility. He had something to gain from it, of course, in both fame and money, but perhaps we should see this from a broader perspective.

Post-war life

Part of Beethoven's career spanned the era when artists saw the first glimmerings of an alternative to the patronage system—that old arrangement in which their livelihoods depended entirely upon pleasing aristocratic employers or others in high places. Now there was some possibility of addressing one's efforts to an emergent public—to unknown persons ready to appreciate and pay for their work. Beethoven operated adroitly in both worlds, striking deals with publishers in several countries, while also cultivating local nobility such as the Lichnowskys and the ever-clinging Archduke Rudolph. The Congress of Vienna simply offered him a particularly rich opportunity to work for a moment within the old system, to do—in a particularly explicit way—what artists, himself included, had always done.

In January 1815, the dignitaries of the Congress gathered at court to celebrate the name day of the Russian Empress. A concert for this occasion featured Beethoven's song "Adelaide," as well as the exultant canon from *Fidelio*, "Mir ist so wunderbar" (meaning, approximately, "I am ecstatic"). Beethoven himself unexpectedly appeared on the stage and agreed to play the piano for this audience of kings and queens, emperors and empresses. He had arrived at the pinnacle of his standing among the elite of all Europe. The singer who performed "Adelaide," Franz Wild, later recalled,

> It would be as untruthful as absurd were I to deny that my vanity was flattered by the distinction which the gathered celebrities bestowed upon me; but the performance of "Adelaide" had one result which was infinitely more gratifying to my artistic nature; it was the cause of my coming into closer contact with the greatest musical genius of all time, Beethoven.

As the Congress continued into the early spring of 1815, old disputes re-emerged about the status of Poland, the division of the Italian peninsula, and other matters. But in March all disagreements were suddenly put aside as word arrived that Napoleon had escaped from Elba and returned to Paris, inaugurating a "Hundred Days" of renewed chaos and uncertainty.

Disillusioned with many aspects of the current restoration, the people gave him a hero's welcome and once more sent Louis XVIII on his travels. Napoleon quickly reassembled an army of some 120,000 and in June led them to the Belgian frontier. After winning two minor battles, he confronted the combined English and Prussian armies at Waterloo and there suffered a massive defeat. This time the Allies were less magnanimous: when the Treaty of Paris was signed on November 1815 and Napoleon had once more abdicated, they pushed France's frontiers back to those of 1790, subjected the country to military occupation, and shipped Napoleon off to St. Helena, an island in the mid-Atlantic, where he died in 1821.

As the "Hundred Days" unfolded in France, the dignitaries in Vienna continued their deliberations, determined to restore Europe to something like its pre-revolutionary state; but they also sought to encourage a balance of power among its major players in the hope of preventing future wars. This determination immediately resulted in closer relations between Austria and England, prompting a noticeable increase in English visitors to Vienna. Among them was the English pianist and composer Charles Neate, aged 30, who arrived hoping to study with Beethoven. Beethoven refused to teach him, but agreed to meet with him occasionally to discuss Neate's compositions. As it worked out, Neate came almost every day, and when Beethoven left for his summer stay at Baden, the young Englishman followed.

Many years later, Neate spoke of that time with Alexander Wheelock Thayer, the distinguished American biographer of Beethoven:

> Nature was like food to him, he seemed really to live in it. Walking in the fields he would sit down on any green bank that offered a good seat, and give his thoughts free course. He was then full of the idea of going to England, but the death of his brother and the adoption of his nephew put an end to the project.

Thayer continued:

> Beethoven, at that time and as Neate knew him, was charmingly good-tempered to those whom he liked—but his dislikes were so strong, that to avoid speaking to persons to whom he was not well affected, he would actually increase his pace in the street to a run. At this time, his dark complexion was very ruddy and extremely animated. His abundant hair was in an admirable disorder. He was always laughing,

when in good humor, which he for the most part was, as Neate saw him. In their conversations Neate spoke clearly and found no difficulty in making himself understood if he spoke into his left ear.

Still, 1815 was not a very productive year for Beethoven. Because he had lost the services of his brother Caspar Carl as business manager and secretary, Beethoven had to conduct most of his voluminous correspondence pen in hand, a significant practical obstacle to writing music. One of the pieces he did finish during the summer was a setting of Goethe's poem, "Meeresstille und glückliche Fahrt" ("Calm Sea and Prosperous Voyage") for chorus and orchestra. It was first performed at his concert in Vienna the following Christmas—and seldom since. That summer he also finished his last two Sonatas for Piano and Cello, Op. 102, apparently intending them as a kind of peace offering to the Countess Erdödy after five years of estrangement. The Countess was an ambitious pianist, and Vienna's premier cellist Joseph Linke was at the time staying at her villa outside the city. These two sonatas continue down the intricate path into the late style begun by the Piano sonata Op. 90, mixing unhurried lyricism with abrupt discontinuities of texture and, at points, stern counterpoint.

In November 1815, Caspar Carl van Beethoven succumbed to tuberculosis. In addition to the "Declaration" of 1813, assigning care of his son Karl to Beethoven, he had signed a later will dividing custody between the composer and the boy's mother Johanna. A court decision then designated the mother as guardian and Beethoven as "associate guardian." Beethoven, in his usual forthright way, took the case to a higher court; citing an earlier judgment of infidelity against Johanna, he appealed for sole custody of Karl and won. He was now the sole caretaker of the nine-year-old boy, an encumbrance that played a central role in the remainder of the composer's life.

7. 1816–1820: More Difficulties

Compositions discussed in the present chapter:

Song cycle "An die ferne Geliebte," Op. 98

Piano Sonata ("Hammerklavier"), Op. 106

Piano sonata, Op. 109

In January 1816, Beethoven's admiring student Charles Neate returned to London with a supply of his master's compositions that he hoped would be performed and published there. Beethoven's other faithful student, Ferdinand Ries, a highly successful pianist and composer then living in London, pursued similar efforts to promote Beethoven's music in that city's vibrant musical scene.

Among the scores Neate took with him were three orchestral overtures that Beethoven had sold to the London Philharmonic Society for a handsome honorarium of 75 guineas (approximately $10,000 in today's money). But the music disappointed members of the Philharmonic Society; they complained that the composer had sent them three *old* overtures when they had expected three newly composed ones, to which they were to have exclusive rights. The Society decided not to perform them. There can be no question that Beethoven had foisted off some of his less useful music (written for past occasions) upon the venerable society. Two of them, *King Stephan* and *The Ruins of Athens*, were composed in 1811 and belonged to the incidental music for plays by August von Kotzebue, performed in Pest (now part of Budapest) in early 1812; the third commemorated the Emperor's name day in 1814.

Still, Beethoven's stock in London musical circles remained high. He dealt at length with a new London publisher, Robert Birchall, who put out a series of his large-scale works in 1816. The following year, the Philharmonic Society offered him a commission for two new symphonies and invited him to London to direct their performance. The society renewed the invitation in the following years; but Beethoven, despite expressions of interest, never felt able to make the trip. Another commission, for an oratorio in one act, came via one of England's most admired musicians, Sir George Smart, conductor of Lenten oratorio performances at Covent Garden and Drury Lane.

Beethoven enjoyed an increasing celebrity status throughout Europe. In 1816, Berlin witnessed a series of triumphal performances of *Fidelio* with the revered soprano Anna Milder-Hauptmann in the title role. And his own Vienna treasured him; whatever his derogatory talk about the place, Viennese journals and newspapers were full of his praise. A leading voice was the respected music critic Friedrich August Kanne, a partisan for the emerging romantic music aesthetic, who placed Beethoven at the center of the newest and best in the art.

In view of all the esteem he enjoyed, Beethoven's day-to-day life during these years might seem rather pedestrian, often petty. He spent many of his waking hours planning the life of his nephew Karl; this consisted in great part of compulsive efforts to prevent him from seeing his mother. Early in 1816, he enrolled Karl in a private boarding school in the city managed by a certain Cajetan Giannatasio del Rio, to whom he wrote:

> It affords me much pleasure to inform you that at last I am bringing you tomorrow the precious pledge that has been entrusted to me. And now I beg you once more under no circumstances to allow his mother to influence him. How or when she is to see him, all this I will arrange with you tomorrow in greater detail—But you yourself must have some sort of watch kept on your servant, *for she has already bribed my servant.*

Then, when the mother made daily attempts to fetch her son after school, Beethoven and Giannatasio petitioned the local court (*Landrecht*) to put a stop to it. Shortly thereafter Beethoven wrote to Giannatasio:

> The Queen of the Night [i.e., the spectacular villainess in Mozart's *Magic Flute*] paid us a surprise visit yesterday and, what is more, uttered a dreadful imprecation upon you. Her usual sauciness and impertinence to me was also displayed on this occasion; it startled me for a moment and almost made me believe that what she stated was the truth. But when I came home later in the day, I received the following decision by order of the *Landrecht* . . . Therefore the boy's mother has to apply to me when she desires to see him.

Notwithstanding all the positive professional attention, in the summer of 1816, Beethoven suffered from poor health and depression, both of which hindered his work. A visitor from Latvia, Dr. Karl von Bursy, who came with a recommendation from the composer's close friend in that country, Karl Amenda, recorded Beethoven's complaints in his diary, interspersing them with his own commentary:

> "I have the misfortune of having all my friends far away from me, and I remain alone in hateful Vienna." . . . He has not been really well for a long time and has composed nothing new . . . He misunderstood me very often, and when I spoke, had to pay the greatest attention in order to understand me. Naturally this troubled and embarrassed me very much . . . He told me a great deal about Vienna and his life here. Venom and rancor raged within him. He defies everything and is dissatisfied with everything and blasphemes against Austria and especially against Vienna.

Later in the summer of 1816, Beethoven managed to spend time at one of his usual rural retreats in the town of Baden. There he received the Giannatasio family who arrived with his nephew Karl. One of the two Giannatasio daughters, Fanny, later wrote,

> We then took a walk through the beautiful Helenenthal, we girls ahead, then Beethoven and our father. What follows we were able to overhear with strained ears: My father thought that B. could rescue himself from his unfortunate domestic conditions only by marriage, did he know anybody, etc. Now our long foreboding was confirmed: he was unhappy in love! Five years ago he had made the acquaintance of a person, a union with whom he would have considered the greatest happiness of his life. It was not to be thought of, almost an impossibility, a chimera—"nevertheless it is now as on the first day."

Thus, four years after the apparent conclusion of the "immortal beloved" episode, it still shadowed Beethoven's mind and was apparently a major cause of his depressed state.

An die ferne Geliebte

Painful memories of his lost love probably motivated Beethoven's major composition project of 1816. That spring he had received a set of poems, *An die ferne Geliebte* ("To the Distant Beloved") from Alois Jeitteles, a 21-year-old physician/poet recently arrived in Vienna. Beethoven immediately set about making them into a *Liederkreis*, or song cycle; during the time of that walk with the Giannatasios near Baden, he was negotiating for its publication.

In German-speaking lands of the mid-18th century, the *Lied* was associated with a passion for primitive, "folk-like" poetry and song. In the latter part of the century, the influential litterateur Johann Gottfried von Herder collected what he believed to be authentic German folk poems and published large numbers of them in 1788-89 as *Stimmen der Völker in Liedern* ("Voices of the People in Song"). Germans at this time thought of the Lied as simple, unpretentious music for amateurs to sing. This "popular" association seems to have kept most of the leading composers of the later 18th century at a distance. Haydn and Mozart both contributed some examples, none of which seem to reflect very serious intent by either composer.

In his more than 50 German songs with piano accompaniment, Beethoven, for the most part, adhered to this "folklike," amateur tradition of the Lied. For example, in his *Geistliche Oden and Lieder* (Sacred Odes and Songs), Op, 48, from 1803–the year of the mighty *Eroica*–he wrote straightforward four-square melodies with plain chordal accompaniments playable by less-skilled musicians.

An die ferne Geliebte, often described as the first song cycle, generally honors this tradition of simplicity, though at emotional high points the piano adds intensity and drama seldom seen in this genre. These six poems, all in regular rhythms, have a single subject: a man's longing for his distant beloved. The clouds, streams, and breezes can go to her, but he cannot; the swallows happily build their nests together, but he remains alone. Beethoven creates the impression of a single work by binding the songs together with short piano interludes. And in the final song, he returns, with some elaboration, to the music of the first. Here, as the generally resigned tone gives way to a more hopeful one ("these songs will dispel that great distance between us"), the tempo increases steadily, ending on a note of triumph.

Beethoven dedicated *An die ferne Geliebte* to his longtime patron Prince Joseph Franz Lobkowitz. This represented the end-point of an extended and, in its latter stages, troubled relationship. Beginning in the 1790s, Lobkowitz had obsessively spent down his family fortune, mainly on music and theater. He even maintained a private orchestra that followed him to and from his various palatial residences in Vienna and Bohemia. Beethoven dedicated many of his major works of the middle period–including the Third, Fifth, and Sixth Symphonies–to Lobkowitz; some of them, including the Third and Fourth Symphonies, were first performed at his home.

As we know, Lobkowitz was one of the three patrons who bestowed that remarkable annuity on Beethoven in 1809. But by 1811 Lobkowitz had accumulated crippling debt; his payments stopped, and Beethoven sued. In 1815, the court held Lobkowitz liable for these payments, and he resumed them. The dedication of *An die ferne Geliebte* to him looks like a gesture of reconciliation. It was too late: Lobkowitz died just as Beethoven was about to send him copies of the printed music.

New piano, Karl, and poor health

Beset with woes in Vienna, Beethoven found the prospect of a sojourn in London ever more attractive. Early in 1818, the Philharmonic Society apparently renewed its offer, and Beethoven wrote to his faithful correspondent there, Ferdinand Ries,

> Despite my desire, it was impossible for me to come to London this year; I beg of you to say to the Philharmonic Society that my poor state of health hindered me; but I hope that I may be entirely well this spring and then take advantage of the renewed offers of the Society towards the end of the year and fulfill all its conditions . . . if it is at all possible I shall get away from here sooner in order to escape total ruin and then will arrive in London in the winter at the latest.

Another sign of the high esteem Beethoven enjoyed in London arrived on his doorstep that spring: a handsome six-and-one half-octave grand piano, a gift from the premier piano manufacturer in England, the firm of John Broadwood & Sons. The instrument traveled by sea to Trieste on the Adriatic, and then bumped along the arduous route over the Alps to Vienna. (Through his highly-placed patron Count Lichnowsky, Beethoven even arranged that the import duty on his expensive gift was forgiven.) Summoning up his best French, he wrote an effusive letter of thanks to Broadwood that translates as: "This piano, with whose presentation you have honored me, I will regard as an altar upon which I will deposit the finest offerings of my spirit to the divine Apollo."

Until this time, Beethoven had owned and played mainly Viennese pianos: instruments with a soft, clear, rather reedy sound and a shallow key dip. The hammers faced back toward the player; the action "flipped" them (instead of '"driving" them) toward the strings. As his hearing declined, Beethoven had often complained of difficulty hearing his piano; he urged his friends, the Viennese pianomakers Johann Andreas and Nannette Streicher, to make him a piano with a sound "as strong as possible."

English grand pianos, with an action resembling that of their modern counterpart, generally had the stronger sound Beethoven was looking for, though pianists used to the Viennese instrument complained of their heavier action and less vibrant sound. Beethoven treasured this instrument and kept it for the rest of his life (refusing to allow Viennese piano technicians even to tune it). When Beethoven died, Franz Liszt acquired the piano and kept it in his Weimar home until his death.

Of the "finest offerings of his spirit" that Beethoven promised Broadwood to "deposit on his piano," this period had little to show. Two main impediments to his work stood in his way: the poor health of which he frequently complained and, far more significant, his obsessive attention to Karl and to measures designed to keep the boy and his mother apart. Just what was wrong with Beethoven's health is hard to discern; frequent references to the matter in his correspondence are never explicit. In January 1818, he began a letter to his remarkably indulgent friend Nanette Streicher, "True, I wrote to you recently that I felt better, but I am not yet quite well. Hence I have not been able to see you." A letter to Ferdinand Ries in London a couple of months later begins, "I am only now recovering from a severe attack from which I have been suffering."

On the other front, the care and keeping of Karl, Beethoven focused mainly on the boy's schooling, how he should be kept occupied at home in Beethoven's chaotic bachelor's household, and how to keep the "Queen of the Night" (Karl's mother) at bay. In May of 1818, as was his habit, Beethoven left Vienna—now with Karl and a pair of servants in tow—for a summer watering-place, this time the Austrian village of Mödling. Once there, he enrolled Karl in a class taught by a local priest, a certain Father Frölich; a month later, the priest dismissed the boy for having reviled his mother—to curry favor, he said, with his current guardian.

The next plan was to place Karl, now nearly 12, in a Viennese public school, which required an entrance examination; so in August of that year they all moved back to the city. But just then the boy's mother petitioned an Austrian court to regain custody. The court's decision in Beethoven's favor placed Karl firmly under his uncle's control, it seemed, and Karl entered the public school in November. But a month later, to Beethoven's horror, the boy ran away and returned to his mother. Beethoven managed to get him back with the help of the police. More court hearings followed in which all three principals testified, Karl saying he would probably prefer to live with his uncle, except that his uncle's deafness made conversation so difficult. Once more the court decided in Beethoven's favor.

The "Hammerklavier" Sonata

Amidst all the turmoil of 1818, Beethoven finished only one big piece: appropriately, it was a piano sonata, the formidable "Hammerklavier" in B♭, Op. 106. We can imagine him at his fine new Broadwood, working out the intricacies of this piece, one of unprecedented length and difficulty.

The sonata opens with what sounds like a peremptory summons: fortissimo chords in a high register with sharply-etched rhythms that seem to brook no opposition. As an answer to this commanding start, we hear something like its opposite: a smooth, contemplative reply comes as if from another world. Permutations and accommodations of these two ideas pervade the movement. But the second of them, ever flexible—though at points growing assertive—comes increasingly to the fore.

Next, an airy scherzo skips along lightly, followed by an *Adagio sostenuto*, likely the longest slow movement Beethoven had ever written, and surely one of his most profound. In the course of its unhurried meditations, we hear stretches of sustained gloom. But there are also moments of relief, a kind of miraculous clearing of the air as the ruling key of F# minor slips quietly into a comforting G major.

Finally, we get the most famous—some might say infamous—part of this composition: a gargantuan fugue that over its protracted course reaches heights of near-manic intensity. A device Beethoven uses to telling effect throughout this movement is the common trill: a fluttering motion that—particularly when it sounds in a low register—simply demands our attention. But just as the Adagio offered moments of respite from its melancholy, this fugue has a quiet place in the middle—*sempre dolce cantabile* (throughout gentle, songful)—where it seems to rest and regroup before the onslaught resumes. In this sonata, particularly in the fugue, Beethoven offered all later pianists an almost insurmountable challenge; this was perhaps the most technically difficult music ever written for the instrument. Its dedicatee, Archduke Rudolph, surely couldn't have played it.

In 1818, that bane of Beethoven's life, his deafness, led him to adopt a novel remedy: the remarkable "conversation books," usually just wads of paper, that he carried with him for others to write down their sides of conversations. At home, friends reported, he often used a slate, where things could be written down and immediately erased. Sometimes, particularly when in public and not wishing to be overheard, Beethoven wrote down his side of conversations as well. And because he was a compulsive saver of almost everything, a great many of these documents have survived, providing a virtually unique record of a historical person's day-to-day exchanges with others. (When they record only the remarks of others, they inspire a sort of parlor game among Beethoven scholars: what must he have said to elicit this reply?)

Fighting for Karl

In 1819, custody struggles over Karl resumed with a vengeance when Viennese officials determined that the earlier hearings had been held in the wrong court, *viz.* the *Landrecht*, which was reserved for litigation among the nobility. (The case had proceeded in the *Landrecht* based upon the false assumption that the Flemish "van" in Beethoven's name was the equivalent of the German "von," a sign of noble lineage.) Now the case went before the City Magistracy, where Beethoven got a much less sympathetic hearing. In February, he pled his case in an astonishingly long and passionate letter to the Magistracy: Karl, he asserted, was receiving a fine education under his direction, with studies in French, drawing, music, and religion, and was about to begin Greek. Further,

> One can see that I have spared no cost in pursuit of the fine goal of presenting to the state a useful and virtuous citizen . . . According to Plutarch, Phillip thought it not a trivial thing to guide the education of his son Alexander himself, and to give him as a teacher the great Aristotle.
>
> Karl's mother, on the other hand, "ridicules him when he tells the truth, yes, even gives him money to pursue lusts and desires that are damaging to him."

In March, Beethoven gave up custody of Karl as the magistrates appeared set to remove him as guardian. What followed was a complex series of adversarial negotiations that finally sent Karl to a private school and, for a time, the guardianship of one Mathias Tuscher. He also spent some months living with his mother. Beethoven attempted persistently to reassert rights of guardianship, even appealing to Archduke Rudolph to act as his advocate. His correspondence and conversation books of the time bear eloquent witness to his near-maniacal immersion in this issue.

In the summer of 1819, Beethoven returned to Mödling, this time in the company of only a single housekeeper. Soon after his arrival, a young music publisher, Moritz Schlesinger, whose family firm was to become dominant in that field for the entire 19th century, visited Beethoven at his summer retreat. His report describes a man ultimately distraught:

> After getting out of the wagon I went to the inn and found Beethoven there, who came out the door in a fury and slammed it hard behind him. After I dusted off a bit I went to the house which was designated as his dwelling. His housekeeper told me that it would be better not to speak to him as he had returned home in a rage. I gave her my visiting card which she brought to him, and after a few minutes to my great astonishment she came out again and bade me enter. There I found the great man at his writing desk . . . He let himself go immediately and told me he was the most miserable man in the world: a minute ago he had come out of the inn where he had asked for a piece of *veal*, which he especially desired; *but there was none there*—all this with a very serious and dark expression.

Early in 1819, the composer's faithful student and benefactor, Archduke Rudolph, had been elected Archbishop of Olmütz (now Olomouc, Czech Republic). For his installation ceremony, scheduled for the following year, Beethoven determined to provide a major composition, declaring: "God will inspire me so that my weak abilities will contribute to the splendor of this festive day." The result, eventually, was the monumental *Missa solemnis* for solo voices, chorus, orchestra, and organ. And whatever his current state of mind, Beethoven apparently worked at it with high energy. He had another visitor that summer in Mödling, the composer's later biographer, Anton Schindler, who arrived with another musician:

> It was four o'clock in the afternoon. As soon as we entered we were told that both Beethoven's maids had left that morning and that there had occurred after midnight an uproar that had disturbed everyone in the house because,

having waited so long, both maids had gone to sleep and the meal they had prepared was inedible. From behind the closed door of one of the parlors we could hear the master working on the fugue of the Credo [of the *Missa Solemnis*], singing, yelling, stamping his feet. When we had heard enough of this almost frightening performance and were about to depart, Beethoven stood before us, his features distorted to the point of inspiring terror . . . His first words were confused, as if he felt embarrassed at having been overheard. Soon he began to speak of the day's events and said, with noticeable self-control, "What a mess! Everyone has run away and I haven't had anything to eat since yesterday noon."

The Archduke's installation as Archbishop took place in March 1820. But Beethoven's big offering for the occasion was far from finished; the first performance of the *Missa solemnis* did not take place until 1824, in St. Petersburg.

Meanwhile, the struggle for Karl ground on into 1820, consuming the lion's share of Beethoven's time and attention. In January, the Magistracy released a detailed ruling in favor of the mother. Beethoven thereupon took the case to an appeals court, proposing joint guardianship with Karl Peters, a friend and a tutor in the Lobkowitz Palace. To this end, he submitted a huge seven-part handwritten document bristling with criticism of the Magistracy, aspersions against Johanna Beethoven (he made much of an illegitimate child she seems to have had in 1811), and claims for his own fitness as guardian. He even made separate appeals in person to the judge and individual members of the court, which, remarkably, the system seems to have permitted those days in Vienna. In July, at last, the court decided in Beethoven's favor: he and Peters were to be joint guardians. Karl remained at Blochinger's school; reports of his progress and behavior now went to Beethoven.

"The highest peaks of musical creation"

In May 1820, Beethoven again retreated to Mödling for another long summer. There he labored diligently on the *Missa solemnis* and began work on his final three piano sonatas, Opp. 109-111. In August, Archduke Rudolph, for whose elevation as Archbishop the unfinished *Missa* had been intended, arrived in Mödling to be near his teacher. Beethoven often complained in private about the time and attention the Archduke required of him; but to the young man himself, a reliable source of income, he always remained elaborately deferential. In September, for example, full of excuses for his recent lack of attentiveness, he wrote to the Archduke in his best self-effacing manner:

> Your Imperial Highness! Since Tuesday evening I have not been well, but believed that by Friday I would be so fortunate as to appear before YIH, but that was a mistake . . . This indisposition came about from my having taken an open post coach in order not to miss YIH. It was a rainy day, and in the evening was practically cold . . . May heaven send all good, beautiful, holy blessings down upon YIH.

Finally back in Vienna toward the end of October, Beethoven received a pair of admiring visitors from Bremen in northern Germany—Wilhelm Christian Müller and his daughter Elise, known as a fine pianist. Shortly after Beethoven's death in March of 1827, Müller published a long, glowing reminiscence about the composer in the *Allgemeine musikalische Zeitung,* based, he said, on years of correspondence with the composer and his friends. Starting with a (generally very accurate) biographical sketch of Beethoven's early life in Bonn, he continued with extended reflections about his life and work. Beethoven, he concluded, had scaled the highest peaks of musical creation. His instrumental compositions simply had the last word in this genre, and Muller predicted that any attempt to extend it further would be futile—a thought that was to haunt many a composer of the following generation.

Financial concerns

During the closing months of 1820 Beethoven, with help from his friends Franz Oliva and Franz Brentano, engaged in energetic correspondence with music publishers about getting his works into print. The not-yet-finished *Missa solemnis* played a prominent role in these dealings: Beethoven loomed so large in the music world that even an unfinished composition of doubtful commercial viability evoked interest among publishers. In correspondence with the Bonn publisher Nikolaus Simrock, Brentano tried to straighten out a tangle of misunderstandings about the various currencies involved in such international transactions: had Simrock promised Beethoven 100 Louis d'or, or was it Friedrichsd'or, or were these the same? In his letter to Simrock at the end of November, Beethoven, ever vigilant about his own financial interest—while denying any concern about such things—entered the fray, starting with an apology for his late reply:

> Since I understand nothing whatever about business affairs, I was waiting for my friend who, however, had not yet arrived in Vienna. Meanwhile I had to learn from other people that I shall be losing at least 100 gulden A. C. With my usual frankness I must confess to you that previously I could have had a fee of 200 gold ducats in Vienna. Yet we gave preference to your offer, because according to the particulars quoted to us 100 Louis d'or were supposed to be worth more . . .

All this haggling about currencies and publication of an unfinished composition turned out to be for naught: Beethoven took nearly two more years to complete the *Missa*, and Simrock never printed it.

This episode shows the mounting investment of energy Beethoven gave to the business side of his life; though friends often lent a helping hand, his career probably suffered substantially.

The year 1820 saw the completion of only one major composition: the fine Piano Sonata in E, Op. 109., dedicated to the 18-year-old Maximiliane, daughter of Antonie and Franz Brentano. The first movement of this remarkable piece begins with a gentle, confident, smooth-flowing passage that is abruptly interrupted, as if by a sudden troubling memory. The music turns improvisatory and darkly uncertain; then, by stages, it smoothes out again as the disturbance seems to resolve, and the opening music returns. We hear one more pair of these starkly opposed moods until, finally, the peaceful one prevails, ending the movement with gentle assurance.

The second movement, prestissimo, opens with jagged rhythmic figures surging upward with unbounded energy. This almost manic motion dominates the movement, relieved only by a quiet interlude in the middle that seems to question what all the fuss is about.

Finally, we get an intriguing set of variations on a quiet, contemplative theme. The construction of the series is various. The first variation suggests simply a continuation of the theme in a higher register; others make use of the repeated halves of this binary theme to produce, in effect, double variations. The final variation unfolds in stages, gaining rhythmic momentum as it at last moves into that trademark texture of Beethoven's late piano music: long, leisurely trills, sometimes in both hands, with figurations abstracted from the theme flowing quietly above and below. And then, to finish where we started, we hear once again the theme itself, understated and unadorned.

8. Adversity and Triumph, 1821-24

*C*ompositions discussed in the present chapter:

"Diabelli" Variations for Piano, Op. 120

Missa Solemnis, Op. 123

Ninth Symphony, Op. 125

During much of 1821, Beethoven was incapacitated from illness. The *Allgemeine musikalische Zeitung* of January 10 reported: "Herr von Beethofen has been sick with a rheumatic fever. All friends of true music and all admirers of his muse feared for him. But now he is on the road to recovery and is actively working again."

But this painted too bright a picture. Three months later, in March, Beethoven wrote to the Berlin publisher Adolf Schlesinger (who was about to publish the Piano Sonata, Op. 109, together with 25 Scottish Songs, Op. 108):

> You may well be thinking badly of me, but you will change your mind when I tell you that for six weeks I have been laid up with a serious rheumatic attack. But now I am doing better. As you can imagine, things came to a standstill; now I will soon catch up with everything . . .

Three months later still, in July, Beethoven wrote, in his usual obsequious tone, to Archduke Rudolph from his summer retreat in the town of Unterdöbling:

> I heard yesterday of Your Highness's arrival here which, however delightful this would otherwise have been for me, has now become for me a sad event, as it may be rather a

long time before I can be so fortunate as to wait on YIH. After being unwell for a long time, I finally suffered a serious case of jaundice—a miserable sickness. I hope that I will be sufficiently recovered at least to see YIH before you leave.

And in another apologetic letter, this one written to Franz Brentano in mid-November, he complained of other afflictions while obliquely apologizing for his late acknowledgment of an advance payment Brentano had sent him for a copy of the (unfinished) *Missa solemnis*. This massive composition continued to occupy most of his attention as he compulsively revised it again and again.

Whatever his distractions and difficulties, during 1821 Beethoven managed to finish the second of his final trio of piano sonatas, the impressive Sonata Op. 110 in A♭, a work known particularly for its gripping fugal finale based on the opening melody of the first movement. The inclusion of rigorous fugal writing in sonata-type movements had become a staple of Beethoven's late style.

One of the best-known episodes of Beethoven's life occurred shortly after his return to Vienna in the fall of 1821. The artist Blasius Höfel described this event years after its occurrence to the eminent Beethoven biographer A. W. Thayer. Höfel was sitting in a tavern in Wiener Neustadt, just outside the city, with friends who included the local police commissioner. It had been after dark, he recalled, when a constable appeared and reported,

> "Mr. Commissioner, we have arrested somebody who will give us no peace. He keeps yelling that he is Beethoven. But he's a tramp: no hat, an old coat, etc." The Commissioner ordered that the man be kept under arrest until the next morning . . . The next day the Commissioner said that about 11 o'clock the previous night a policeman had awakened him to report that the prisoner would not calm down . . . . So the Commissioner got up, dressed, went out and woke up Herzog [a local musician], and in the middle of the night took him to the jail. Herzog, as soon as he looked at the man, exclaimed, "That *is* Beethoven!" . . . As it happened,

Beethoven had got up early in the morning, slipped on a miserable old coat and, without a hat, had gone out for a little walk. He got on the towpath of the canal and walked on and on. He seemed to have lost his way, for, with nothing to eat, he had continued on until he ended up at the canal basin at the Ungerthor. Here, not knowing where he was, he was seen looking in the windows of houses. As he looked so like a beggar the people had called a constable who arrested him. Upon his arrest the composer said, "I am Beethoven." "Of course, why not"? said the policeman. "You're a tramp. Beethoven doesn't look like this."

When he wandered beyond his usual haunts, Beethoven encountered recognition of his fame, it seems, but not of his eccentricities.

Strained family ties

Familial relations, too, rocked the creative boat a bit in this period. In the decade after Beethoven's visit with his brother Johann in Linz in 1812, and his rather high-handed attempt to interfere with Johann's personal life (see Chapter 6), the brothers apparently had little contact. During those years, Johann's pharmaceutical business flourished; he invested extensively in real estate and began to spend his winters in Vienna. In 1822, Beethoven proposed that the two of them share an apartment, but eventually moved into a house adjoining the home where Johann, his wife Therese, and her daughter Amalie spent their winters. In this close proximity, they led an uneasy existence; Beethoven eyed Johann with a certain suspicion and some contempt, even as he accepted business advice and loans from him.

Gerhard von Breuning, son of Beethoven's old friend Stephan von Breuning, remembered Johann thus:

> He was not exactly tall, but much taller than Ludwig. His

nose was large and rather long, the position of his eyes, crooked, the effect being as if he squinted a little with one eye. The mouth was crooked, one corner drawn upwards giving him the expression of a mocking smile. In his garb he affected a well-to-do elegant, but the role did not fit his angular, bony figure.

Beethoven's friends and associates also tended to view Johann with some disdain, seeing him as pretentious and eager to bask in the reflected glory of his famous brother. Count Lichnowsky wrote in a conversation book, "Everybody thinks him a fool . . . all the world says of him that his only merit is that he bears your name." Beethoven himself once referred to him as "asinaccio" (bastardized Italian for "stupid one"). And in 1823, Johann's wife Therese once again sparked Beethoven's anger; Schindler stirred this pot by writing to Beethoven that Therese had quite ignored Johann when he was ill, and even openly brought a lover to their home. Beethoven told Schindler to bring in the police and (futilely) urged his brother to have nothing more to do with his wife or her daughter.

Meeting Rossini

Beethoven also had to contend with competition on the musical front. In late March 1822, the newest sensation of the Italian opera scene, Gioachino Rossini, arrived in Vienna with an Italian opera company for what was to be a triumphant season at the principal opera theater of the city, the Kärntnertortheater. There, Viennese audiences heard seven of Rossini's works, including serious operas such as Zelmira and Elisabetta, Regina d'Inghilterra (Elizabeth, Queen of England). The season was a triumphant success—particularly so were those works that featured Rossini's new wife, the renowned soprano Isabella Colbran.

Rossini greatly admired the much older Beethoven and met with him at least once during his visit. What transpired there, strangely enough, we know only from an account of a much later conversation between Rossini and Richard Wagner. Beethoven, Wagner reported, had congratulated Rossini for Il Barbiere di Siviglia (The Barber of Seville) and urged him to concentrate on opera buffa (Italian comic opera). Beethoven opined that opera buffa was the ideal genre for Italian composers because they were not qualified, either by temperament or musical training, to deal with truly dramatic subjects. Rossini seems to have taken this slur in good grace. What really impressed him about this meeting were the wretched conditions under which Beethoven lived. Later that evening, at a dinner with Prince Metternich and other members of the Austrian nobility, Rossini urged them to provide financial relief for "the greatest genius of our age." The assembled aristocrats reacted negatively, believing that the misanthropic and surly Beethoven had only himself to blame.

Beethoven and his circle did not reciprocate Rossini's admiration. At a concert of Beethoven's music in 1824, the theater manager insisted on including an aria of Rossini's on the program—between the Kyrie of the *Missa solemnis* and the Ninth Symphony, the audience was to hear the tenor aria "Di tanti palpiti" from Rossini's Tancredi. Beethoven's nephew Karl observed, "Some people stayed away because they felt indignant at the inclusion of that aria . . . this can do you no harm, except that some may be outraged that your compositions should be profaned by being placed, in effect, in the same class as Rossini's 'tootlings.'" Beethoven purportedly said later that Rossini had a real talent, especially for melody, but that his music illustrated the frivolous and sensuous spirit of the time.

"Unscrupulous" negotiations

In mid-1822 Beethoven began negotiations with a new music publisher, C. F. Peters of Leipzig. In a long letter to Peters of June 5, he waxed rather poetic about the principles that should govern such negotiations:

> I love straightforwardness and uprightness and am of the opinion that the artist ought not to be slighted; for alas! glittering as is the external aspect of fame, he is not permitted to be Jupiter's guest on Olympus every day; too often and too repulsively vulgar mankind drags him down from the ethereal heights.

He offered Peters a long list of his compositions including "the biggest work I have written up until now, a great mass with chorus, four soloists obbligato, and large orchestra"–i.e., the as yet incomplete *Missa solemnis*.

Peters promptly agreed to publish the *Missa* and several other compositions on condition that he should have exclusive rights to them. Beethoven agreed, promising to dispatch the music by August 15; Peters sent him a substantial honorarium in return. By late December, however, and after repeated enquiries, Peters had received nothing. Beethoven claimed delays in copying. As these negotiations dragged on into 1823, he tried to appease Peters with a few songs and bagatelles, meanwhile offering the *Missa solemnis* to at least three other publishers. In the end, Peters returned the music he had received and published nothing of Beethoven's.

There can be little question about it: in his dealings with Peters Beethoven had been "dragged down from his ethereal heights"–not by "vulgar mankind," but by himself. In short, he was unscrupulous. One might cite extenuating circumstances: he was under worrying financial pressure for the care of nephew Karl; he already owed money to two other music publishers and presently would be indebted to brother Johann as well. But in this and one or two other cases from this period, Beethoven cut himself a good bit of slack.

Beethoven and Schubert

In the summer of 1822, Beethoven had several meetings with Friedrich Rochlitz, the greatly respected poet and music critic, editor of the musical journal, *Allgemeine musikalische Zeitung*. Rochlitz, a warm admirer of Beethoven—but also, in the composer's view, sometimes annoyingly critical of him—left a detailed account of these meetings. His recollection reinforces the impression that Beethoven showed a wide range of changing moods. Prior to one meeting, Rochlitz had spoken with Beethoven's much younger contemporary and fellow Vienna resident, Franz Schubert.

> "If you wish to see him in a more natural and jovial mood" said Schubert, "then go right now and eat your dinner at the inn where he has just gone." Schubert took me with him. Most of the places were taken. Beethoven sat among several acquaintances who were strangers to me . . . I found a seat from which I could see him and, since he spoke loud enough, also could hear nearly all that he said. It could not actually be called a conversation, for he spoke in monologue . . . Those about him contributed little, merely laughing or nodding their approval. He philosophized, or, one might even say, politicized, after his own fashion. He spoke of England and the English, and about how he associated both with a splendor incomparable . . . Then he told all sorts of stories of the French, from the days of the second occupation of Vienna. For them he had no kind words. His remarks were all made with unconcern and without the least reserve. And whatever he said was spiced with highly original, naïve judgments and comical fancies.
>
> Later, Rochlitz notes, he and Beethoven—with the help of a tablet—conversed at length, the composer launching into a diatribe about the lack of appreciation he found in Vienna: "You will hear nothing of me here . . . *Fidelio*? They cannot give it, nor do they want to listen to it. The symphonies?

They have no time for them. My concertos? Everyone grinds out only the stuff he himself has made." Next the talk turns to Goethe: "It was at Karlsbad that I made his acquaintance—God only knows how long ago! At that time I was not altogether deaf as I am now, though I heard with great difficulty. And what patience the great man had with me!" He told numerous anecdotes and gave the most enjoyable details.

Rochlitz continues:

Our third meeting was the merriest of all. He came here, to Baden, this time looking quite neat, clean, even elegant. Yet this did not prevent him—it was a warm day—from taking a walk in the Helenenthal. This means on the road that all travel, even the Emperor and Imperial family, and where everyone crowds past everyone else on the unusually narrow path. There he took off his fine black frockcoat, slung it across his shoulder from a stick, and wandered along in his shirtsleeves. He stayed from about ten in the forenoon until six o'clock in the evening . . . During the entire visit he was uncommonly gay and at times most amusing. All that entered his mind had to come out. "Well, it happens that I am unbuttoned today," he said, and the remark was entirely in order.

One local music publisher to whom Beethoven offered the *Missa solemnis* was Anton Diabelli. Diabelli, also a composer and guitar teacher, had gone into business in Vienna in 1817; he soon became an important supporter of Schubert, publishing his (later famous) songs "Gretchen am Spinnrade" and "Erlkönig" in 1821. Beethoven evidently took a liking to Diabelli, partly because his name offered an obvious opportunity for a (somewhat lame) pun: Beethoven called him Diabolus Diabelli. In 1819, Diabelli had composed a little waltz and invited all the Austrian composers he could think of to contribute single variations on it. The idea was to publish an anthology of variation types with a patriotic caste (as the waltz was thought distinctly Viennese): it was to be called *Vaterländischer Künstlerverein* (Artists' Union of the Fatherland). Fifty composers contributed one variation each; among them were Czerny, Schubert, Hummel, Archduke Rudolph, and the very youthful Liszt. Beethoven first declined to participate but in the end sent not one, but 33 variations. As this unexpected contribution hardly fit his plan, Diabelli published Beethoven's composition separately—with the added benefit of affixing his own name to them for all posterity.

Keyboard variations and *Fidelio*

Since the time of Mozart, keyboard variations had been an omnipresent fixture of amateur music. Variations on operatic arias were particularly popular: they allowed one, after attending an operatic performance, to recreate a similar experience at home. Beethoven wrote many sets of variations clearly intended for the delectation of amateur pianists. But he also at times invested his best efforts in the genre, producing music of great originality and complexity, as, for example, in the Piano Variations, Op. 35 (based on the same tune as the finale of the "Eroica" Symphony) of 1802. The *Diabelli Variations*—perhaps in response to Bach's *Goldberg Variations*, which Beethoven likely knew—also vastly transcend the level of music intended for amateur players.

Diabelli's waltz is an amiable little dance in the expected triple meter whose two halves end with repeated three-note upward gestures that Beethoven at first ridiculed as *Schusterflecke* (cobbler's patches—apparently, bits of leather used to repair holes in shoes). Beethoven's first variation, *alla Marcia maestoso* in quadruple meter, while clearly referring to that theme, inhabits quite a different expressive sphere. The variations that follow present a veritable anthology of keyboard styles: the 10th one features perpetual motion ranging over the entire available keyboard; the 13th is spare in the extreme, with terse two- or three-note gestures separated by great yawning rests; the 24th and 32nd are fugues. Variation 22 cleverly plays on the theme's resemblance to "Notte e giorno faticar" that opens Mozart's *Figaro*—Beethoven includes a verbal heading to make sure we don't miss the point.

In November of 1822, Beethoven's complaint to Rochlitz about Viennese audiences' indifference to *Fidelio* met with a welcome contradiction. A run of seven performances with Wilhelmine Schröder (later internationally famous as Schröder-Devrient) in the title role was a huge success. But there were troubles along the way. Beethoven's friends feared that the deaf composer might wish to conduct the performances himself, and they were right. Shortly before the opening night, Beethoven announced that he would, in fact, conduct. At the rehearsal—it was, astonishingly, commonplace at the time to hold only one—the overture went reasonably well. But soon things began to fall apart: during the first duet (Rocco and Leonore), Schindler recalled, the singers and the orchestra proceeded at different tempos, and there was mass confusion about repetitions. So, Schindler continued,

> I approached him in the orchestra. He handed me his notebook, asking that I write down what the trouble was. Quickly I wrote, in effect, "Please do not continue—more at home." With a bound he was in the parterre, saying, "Out, quick!". . . In his lodgings he threw himself on the sofa, covered his face with his hands . . . at dinner not a word escaped from his lips; he was a picture of melancholy and depression.

In later years Schröder-Devrient described that rehearsal in more graphic terms:

> Beethoven sat in the orchestra and waved his baton over everyone's heads . . . At that time the master's ear was already closed to all sounds. With a bewildered face and unearthly inspired eyes, waving his baton back and forth with violent motions, he stood in the midst of the perform-

ing musicians and didn't hear a note! If he thought it should be piano, he crouched down almost under the conductor's desk, and if he wanted forte he jumped up with the strangest gestures, uttering the weirdest sounds.

But in the end, with the composer-conductor Ignaz Umlauf at the helm, the performances were by all accounts a splendid success. One member of the audience at the second performance was a young musician from Darmstadt, later a well-known composer, Louis Schlösser. His recollections illustrate the esteem Beethoven enjoyed by this time in the musical world. In his "Personal Reminiscences of Beethoven," written about 50 years later, he recalled leaving the theater with his friend Franz Schubert. Three men walked ahead of them.

> Then Schubert very softly plucked my sleeve, pointing to the gentleman in the middle, who turned his head at that moment so that the bright light of the lamps fell on it. I saw, familiar to me from engravings and paintings, the features of the creator of the opera I had just heard, Beethoven himself. My heart beat twice as loudly . . . I remember that I followed the Esteemed One and his companions (Schindler and Breuning, as I later learned) like a shadow through crooked alleys and past high, gable-roofed houses until the darkness hid him from sight.

Later, Schlösser made several vain attempts to visit Beethoven. Finally, having won the task of delivering a letter from the Hessian Court about a subscription to the *Missa solemnis*, he simply walked into Beethoven's home:

> I entered and found myself in a rather spacious but quite undecorated apartment. A large, square oak table with various chairs, which presented a somewhat chaotic aspect, stood in the middle of the room. On it lay writing-books and lead pencils, music paper and pens, a chronometer, a

metronome, an ear-trumpet made of yellow metal, and various other things. On the wall at the left of the door was the bed, completely covered with musical scores and manuscripts. I recall a framed oil-painting (it was a portrait of Beethoven's grandfather, for whom, as is known, he had a child-like reverence) which was the only decoration I noticed . . .

I apparently arrived shortly after he had eaten breakfast, for he repeatedly passed the napkin lying beside him over his snow-white teeth—a habit of his, incidentally, which I frequently observed . . . Just about to explain the reason for my visit, I fortunately recalled the uselessness of speaking, and reverentially handed him the letter with its great seal.

Beethoven seized his ear-trumpet, and I explained the unbounded veneration with which his works were received, with what enthusiasm they were heard, and what an influence the perfection of his creations had on the cultural level of the time. Though Beethoven was not susceptible to flattery of any kind, my words, coming from the depths of my soul, seemed to touch him, and this led me to tell him of my nocturnal pursuit of him after the performance of *Fidelio*. "But what prevented you from coming to see me in person?," he asked. "I am sure you have heard a good bit of contradictory nonsense—that I am seen as an edgy, capricious, arrogant sort, whose music one might enjoy, but who as a person is best avoided . . . I meet few people who understand my thoughts and feelings, so content myself with just a few friends."

Schlösser met Beethoven once more in Vienna, this time at the music shop of Steiner and Haslinger. "At this encounter," Schlosser wrote,

I was at the outset so surprised to see Beethoven, usually so careless about his attire, dressed with unusual elegance: a blue frock coat with yellow buttons, impeccable white knee-breeches, a vest to match, and a new beaver hat worn, as usual, on the back of his head . . . I could not resist telling my teacher [Joseph] Meyseder about the striking metamorphosis in Beethoven's appearance . . . He said, with a smile, 'This is not the first time his friends have taken away his old clothes during the night and put down new ones in their place; he has not the least suspicion of what has happened and puts on whatever lies before him.'"

Playing at royal courts and other honors

After the collapse of negotiations with Peters for the publication of the *Missa solemnis*, Beethoven pursued a different tack: instead of dealing with a single publisher, he proceeded to offer handmade copies of the composition to a series of sovereign European courts, for a hefty price, to allow its performance at exalted venues around Europe before publication. (One or two local performances of a big new piece were not unusual, but such a wide dispersal—for money—of a composition in advance of publication was surely novel.) Schindler was in charge of the correspondence, and—adopting a suitably servile manner—wrote to many ruling courts in German-speaking lands, plus those in Paris, Copenhagen, St. Petersburg, and Tuscany. The letter, which Beethoven signed, ended, "Since, however, the copying of the score necessitates considerable expense, the undersigned ventures most humbly to inform your royal highness that for this great work he has fixed the moderate fee of 50 ducats; and he flatters himself that he will enjoy the exceptional honor of being allowed to count Your Royal Highness among the number of his distinguished subscribers."

Beethoven reinforced these efforts by enlisting Archduke Rudolph to write supporting letters to the Saxon and Tuscan courts; to improve prospects at the Ducal Court of Weimar, Beethoven himself wrote to its most distinguished resident, Goethe. Ten courts immediately accepted this remarkable proposal, among them those of Saxony, Russia, and Prussia. King Louis XVIII of France, just entering the final year of his tenuous reign, not only subscribed to the *Missa solemnis*, but also sent Beethoven a gold medal with the engraving "Doné par le Roi à Monsieur Beethoven," prompting Beethoven to write him a long letter in laborious French. A representative from the Court of Vienna asked Beethoven if he would not prefer a "royal order" to the 50 ducats, to which the composer responded without hesitation, "50 ducats."

Another honor had come Beethoven's way in December 1822: the Royal Academy of Music in Stockholm elected him to its membership, subject to the approval of the Austrian authorities. This finally happened the following spring, leading Beethoven to write two more effusive letters in French, one to the Royal Academy, the other to the then King of Sweden and Norway, Karl XIV. King Karl had been born in France as Jean Baptiste Bernadotte, and for a brief time in 1798 had served as the French ambassador in Vienna. In that role (if we are to credit Schindler) he had received Beethoven and suggested that he compose a symphony in honor of Napoleon, thus planting the seeds of the *Eroica*.

In the spring of 1823, Beethoven had contact with another star in the musical firmament of the following generation. Carl Czerny's sensational young pupil Franz Liszt, age 11, came to town for a concert. A few days before, Schindler introduced the boy and his father to Beethoven. An entry in a conversation book (probably written by the father) appeals to Beethoven on Liszt's behalf in stilted language: "I have often expressed the desire to Herr Schindler to make your high acquaintance, and am delighted to be able to do so now. On Sunday the 13th I shall give a concert, and most humbly beg you to honor me with your exalted presence." According to Liszt's later recollection, Beethoven did attend the concert; afterwards he went on the stage, lifted up the prodigy, and kissed him.

Missa solemnis performed at last

Ever-present in Beethoven's thoughts in the early 1820s was his biggest project of the time, the majestic *Missa solemnis*. The first performance of the entire work finally took place on April 18, 1824, not in Vienna, but in St. Petersburg, under the sponsorship of Prince Nikolay Galitzin—who would soon become a force in Beethoven's career. The following month, as we have mentioned, sections of the mass (in the company of a Rossini aria) were performed in Beethoven's concert at the Court Theater in Vienna; but the entire work was not heard in Austria until 1830, so that Beethoven never witnessed the composition performed whole. Nor did he ever see it in print; its publication, by Schott in Mainz, occurred shortly after the composer's death in the spring of 1827.

Except for the opera *Fidelio*, the *Missa Solemnis*—requiring four soloists, chorus, a large orchestra, and organ, and lasting about 80 minutes—is Beethoven's biggest piece, and more than once he cited it as his greatest achievement. As early as the summer of 1822, when the work was still very much in progress, he declared to his pupil Ferdinand Ries, "My greatest work is a grand mass, which I have just written." Up to this time he had composed only one mass, the rather modest Mass in C of 1807. But beginning in mid-1819, in dead earnest about preparing for his new task, Beethoven pursued various antiquarian studies. In the Archduke's library, he pored over examples of polyphonic masses from the 16th century to his own time. He studied the church modes of medieval plainsong and sought traditional theoretical works on church music. But he apparently also thought of this composition as transcending the bounds of liturgical music: in several letters to potential subscribers, he stressed that the *Missa* could also be performed outside a church setting as an oratorio.

Over the centuries, the Catholic mass had presented well-known difficulties for composers. Standard practice prescribed composing only the texts of the "Ordinary," i.e., the five sections of the mass that were sung at services throughout the church year. But these constitute an ill-assorted group of texts: the *Kyrie* and *Agnus dei* are short and poetic, while the *Gloria* and *Credo* are long and mainly prosodic, and the Sanctus lies somewhere in between. Beethoven determined to overcome such obstacles, even as he set up new ones for himself, particularly with an imposing array of fugal writing. (When Schindler had heard Beethoven "working on the fugue of the *Credo*, singing, yelling, stamping his feet," the music in question was more likely the gargantuan fugue at the end of the *Gloria*–beginning with the words "In Gloria Dei Patris"–a technical tour-de-force with few equals in Western music.)

At points in this work, Beethoven adopted unconventional procedures that seemed to have a personal significance for him. In the *Agnus Dei*, the final words are a plea, "Dona nobis pacem" (Grant us peace). Above the musical staves, Beethoven wrote "Bitte um innern und äussern Frieden" (Prayer for inner and outer peace). After a bit of appropriately pastoral music, however, he summoned the idea of peace by invoking its opposite. Military trumpet calls sound from the orchestra as earlier bits of the text reappear, particularly "miserere nobis" (have mercy on us). This plea is now associated with struggle and war, those constant companions of Beethoven's earlier life. But presently pastoral music returns with repetition of "Dona nobis pacem," leading to a triumphant fugue (whose subject Beethoven seems to have borrowed from the Hallelujah Chorus of Handel's *Messiah*). Peace, in its broadest sense, Beethoven evidently saw as a positive and powerful thing; a prayer for its realization becomes a fitting climax to this monumental work.

Why did Beethoven invest such prodigious effort in composing the "Ordinary" of the Catholic mass, carrying on with the project after its ostensible motivation–the Archduke's elevation–had vanished, and regarded the result as his greatest work? He was not driven, surely, by religious zeal: Beethoven was a nominal Catholic, but, from his early years in Bonn, he paid scant attention to the church, showing much more interest in the rationalist and humanist thought of the Enlightenment that flourished around him. Still, especially in later life, he showed powerful, if scattered, signs of religious feeling. At times he was drawn to various strains of Eastern mysticism. But he showed a more sustained allegiance to pantheistic thought—a belief in the presence of God in all nature—as represented in the then-popular writings of Christoph Christian Sturm (1740-86). And shortly before beginning work on the *Missa solemnis*, Beethoven gave an approving nod to something closer to traditional Catholicism: he proposed entrusting Karl's education to Professor Johann Michael Sailer, later Bishop at Regensburg. Though highly placed in the Church hierarchy, Sailer advocated a personal sort of Christian belief quite separate from Catholic liturgy and worship. Beethoven's religious impulses were as varied as they were strong.

The early 1820s were a time of growing international honor and attention for Beethoven. But the problems and annoyances of his ordinary life persisted. In the late summer of 1823, after quarrels with his landlord, Beethoven determined to move from Hetzendorf (then just outside Vienna) to his favorite resort town, Baden; he dispatched Schindler to arrange for a place to stay. The Baden landlord from a previous summer, however, refused to rent to the composer until he received "a promise of better order and respect for other occupants." Furthermore, Schindler said, "One specific stipulation . . . was made, that in order to have the room overlooking the street as in past years, Beethoven must provide it with window shutters. We tried in vain to learn the reason for this strange demand." The reason, it turned out, had to do with Beethoven's habit of scrawling all kinds of memoranda on his shutters in lead pencil—accounts, musical themes, etc. A family from North Germany had noticed this in the previous year and had bought one of the shutters as a memento. The thrifty landlord had an eye for business and disposed of the remaining shutters to other visitors."

Failed projects

The successful revival of *Fidelio* in the fall of 1822 rekindled

Beethoven's interest in finding another good opera subject. Count Lichnowsky persuaded the young Viennese dramatist Franz Grillparzer (1791-1872), just then celebrated for works recently performed at the Burgtheater, to produce a libretto for Beethoven. The resulting work, *Melusine*, drew upon well-known European folklore about a mermaid-like water sprite and her exploits. In the summer of 1823, Grillparzer sent the libretto to Beethoven, who seemed to approve and agreed to meet and discuss the matter. Of his and Schindler's visit to Beethoven's lodgings, Grillparzer recalled: "As we entered Beethoven arose from the bed, gave me his hand, poured out his feelings of goodwill and respect and at once broached the subject of the opera. 'Your work lives here,' he said, pointing to his heart. 'I am going to the country in a few days, and shall at once begin to compose it.'" Beethoven even proposed that the two of them sign a contract about dividing the profits from the opera; he reportedly also pursued contract negotiations for the opera's performance with the management of the Kärntnertortheater. But nothing ever came of this project; not a single sketch for the opera survives among Beethoven's papers.

Another project from this period also never came to fruition: an oratorio that Beethoven had agreed to write in 1819 for the prestigious Vienna Gesellschaft der Musikfreunde (Society of the Friends of Music), and for which he had accepted a substantial honorarium in advance. The work, *Der Sieg des Kreuzes* ("The Victory of the Cross"), drew upon a legend about the fourth-century Roman emperor Constantine the Great. This legend had it that in a battle for Rome against his opponent Maxentius, Constantine experienced a vision of the cross with the inscription "In hoc signo vinces" ("Through this sign you conquer"), and conquer he did. Beethoven's friend Karl Bernard agreed to write the libretto but didn't finish it until the fall of 1823. Responding to an exasperated letter from the Gesellschaft in early 1824, Beethoven blamed his delinquency on dissatisfaction with Bernard's work ("I would rather set Homer, Klopstock, Schiller to music"), and suggested the Gesellschaft might perform the oratorio-like *Missa solemnis* instead. There is no sign that Beethoven ever did any actual work on *Der Sieg des Kreuzes*—nor that he returned his advance.

As the Gesellschaft waited in vain for Beethoven's oratorio in 1823, his thoughts lay elsewhere: first, he wished to complete the *Missa solemnis*, and then to turn to his other big project of the time, the Ninth Symphony. This famous work, the first symphony to feature solo and choral singing—which at the time seemed a contradiction of terms—evolved torturously. It resulted, basically, from the confluence of three separate projects: two symphonies and a setting of Schiller's Ode, "An die Freude" ("To Joy").

Ode to Joy

While at work on the Seventh and Eighth Symphonies in 1812, Beethoven formed plans for another pair. He wrote notes to himself about a "Symphony in D minor" (the key of the Ninth). In 1818, he proposed introducing voices into a symphony that was to follow the one in D minor: "Pious song in a symphony in the ancient modes . . . The whole 2d symphony might be characterized in this manner in which case the vocal parts would enter in the last movement or already in the Adagio." He had expressed an interest in composing Schiller's poem, that paean to the solidarity of all humankind, as early as 1793 and several times thereafter. But it was not until 1822 when plans for the two new symphonies had become one, and the Ninth was well underway, that he showed any intention of incorporating the Ode as a choral finale.

The idea posed a vexing challenge: how to introduce vocal parts into the finale after the singers had sat mute on the stage during the first three movements. Schindler recalled an event from the fall of 1823:

> "One day [Beethoven] burst into the room and shouted at me: 'I have it! I have it!' He held his sketchbook out to me

so that I could read: 'Let us sing the song of the immortal Schiller'; then a solo voice began the Hymn of Joy."

That inspiration required a good bit of elaboration. In the final version of the symphony, Beethoven opens the fourth movement with an outraged, dissonant flurry of sound in all the wind instruments, as if the music struggles to surmount some formidable barrier. What follows shows what that barrier is: the conceptual chasm between the musical expression of instrumental sound alone and that which also makes use of words and the human voice.

The cellos and basses play then an unmistakably clear imitation of dramatic recitative—a discourse that hovers between speech and song. After repeating this procedure, Beethoven quotes, in turn, the openings of the symphony's three preceding movements, each time cut off abruptly by the imperious recitative-like statement of the cellos and basses. Finally, the orchestra hesitantly advances an entirely new theme, which those tyrannical low strings accept and play in full. Little by little the other instruments join in for a triumphant statement of this "new-found" theme.

This is all very mysterious, and Beethoven begins anew as if to explain himself. He offers a shortened repetition of all these proceedings, omitting the quotations from preceding movements; but now the recitative-like parts are actual recitative, sung by the baritone soloist. The words are apparently Beethoven's own: "O friends, not these tones; instead let us sing more pleasing and joyful ones." The "more joyful tones," of course, are that new theme, which the baritone now sings to the first lines of Schiller's poem (given here in literal translation):

> Freude, schöner Götterfunken, (Joy, of fine divine spark)
>
> Tochter aus Elysium, (Thou daughter from Elysium)
>
> Wir betreten feuertrunken, (Fire-drunken we approach)
>
> Himmlische, dein Heiligtum (Heavenly one, thy holiness.)

> Deine Zauber binden wider (Thine enchantments bind together)
>
> Was die Mode streng geteilt, (What fashion has rent asunder,)
>
> Alle Menschen werden Brüder (All people become brothers)
>
> Wo dein sanfter Flügel weilt. (Where thy gentle wing tarries.)

This becomes the first in a magnificent series of variations on the Freude theme with ever-changing antiphonal effects among soloists, chorus, and orchestra. And the military allusion in the exhortation "Follow your path with joy, Brothers, like a hero marching to victory," inspired Beethoven to offer a variation in the style of "Turkish Music"—a common European imitation of the sound of drums, triangles, and cymbals in the military music of the reputedly ferocious Turks.

A second big section of the movement uses the ecstatic concluding stanza of Schiller's poem:

> Seid umschlungen, Millionen! (Be embraced, you millions!)
>
> Diesen Kuss der ganzen Welt! (This kiss to the whole world!)
>
> Brüder—überm Sternenzelt (Brothers, above the starry canopy)
>
> Muss ein lieber Vater wohnen. (A loving father must dwell.)

Such expansive sentiments of mingled humanistic and religious enthusiasm surely appealed to the composer, and he set these words to a soaring melody in the second big section of the movement. And then, in the final part—perhaps predictably—we get a wonderfully intricate combination of the two main themes, a marriage of Joy and Brotherhood.

Each of the three earlier movements from which Beethoven quotes in that finale is a highly individual creation conceived on a grand scale. The first movement seems to begin in a void with something akin to lightning bolts descending in the distance; the agitation draws closer and arrives as a hugely forceful descending figure suggestive of unfolding cataclysm. We hear several other themes, some nearly lyrical; but at the moment of recapitulation, that alarming opening returns, and the overall impression of the movement remains one of titanic power barely under control. Then comes a scherzo abounding in energy and shot through with imitative, quasi-fugal textures; all this hyper-activity relaxes in the middle with a much calmer trio. Next is an expansive Adagio built upon two themes: the first sounds sober and contemplative; the second soars upward again and again with fine, optimistic abandon. But now Beethoven wishes to make an aesthetic point. All this marvelous music, he seems to say at the start of the finale, constitutes merely a springboard for the main point of the symphony: to break out of the bounds of pure music and include voices, words, and ideas, to celebrate things like brotherhood and joy with new explicitness.

When Beethoven finally finished the score of the Ninth Symphony in February 1824, he suffered profound uncertainty about what he had wrought. Was that choral finale a terrible mistake? (Schiller, incidentally, had long since discounted his "An die Freude" as youthful folly.) Would the fickle Viennese public, presently caught up in the Rossini craze, have any interest in a work of this immensity and seriousness? When an inquiry with a friend in Berlin about a performance of the mass and symphony there received a positive response, several of Beethoven's highly-placed friends, led by Prince Lichnowsky, wrote him a long and worshipful plea that the new symphony be premiered in Vienna.

After exhaustive reassurances, plans, and negotiations pursued by his friends, Beethoven finally agreed to a concert in the Kärntnertortheater in May, with the Ninth, three movements of the *Missa solemnis*, and the Overture *Die Weihe des Hauses* (Dedication of the House) on the program. (As the censors forbade the performance of mass movements in an opera theater, the printed program disguised them as "grand hymns.") Then came the ticklish question about Beethoven's participation in the concert. The solution provided that Michael Umlauf and Beethoven would both conduct—though Umlauf quietly instructed the musicians to pay no attention to Beethoven. Years later, the pianist Sigismund Thalberg recalled that concert:

> Beethoven was dressed in a black dress-coat [another report claimed it was green], white neckerchief, and waistcoat, black satin small-clothes, black silk stockings, shoes with buckles. After the Scherzo of the Ninth Symphony B. stood turning over the leaves of his score, utterly deaf to the immense applause, and Unger [Karoline Unger, soprano soloist] pulled him by the sleeve, pointed to the audience; then he turned and bowed.

Whatever Beethoven's doubts about his last symphony, this work has inspired speculation, interpretation—and sometimes manipulation—ever since. Wagner saw it as a crucial cementing of an alliance between word and music that opened the way to his own grand project of the music drama. Composers of symphonies after Beethoven—Schumann, Brahms, Mahler—could not escape the nagging suspicion that Beethoven had said the last word in that genre: that the Ninth had essentially closed the symphonic genre down.

Since its creation, the Ninth has served many, sometimes conflicting, artistic and political points of view. During World War II, both sides used the Ninth as a rallying cry—the Nazis, of course, needing to clarify in accompanying commentary that Schiller's and Beethoven's "brotherhood" did not include *everybody*—only Aryans. Leonard Bernstein famously performed the symphony in 1989 to celebrate the tearing down of the Berlin Wall; for this occasion, Schiller's *Freude* was replaced by the more apposite *Freiheit* (freedom). The Ninth has even become the object of feminist disapproval: musicologist Susan McClary, for example, described the symphony's opening as an outpouring of "horrifyingly violent masculine rage." So this work has seemed readily adaptable to many divergent points of view.

But Beethoven created it, and his listeners first heard it, within a particular political and social context: life under the repressive Metternich regime, a government intent upon suppressing any lingering notions of social equality and personal freedoms left over from French Revolutionary and Napoleonic times. We know of Beethoven's opposition to that state of affairs; the throngs of listeners who cheered his celebration of freedom and joy surely did as well.

The Viennese public had one more chance to hear Beethoven's new creation: a second concert, later in May 1824, repeated the Ninth and the mass movements. But at the theater management's instigation—and to the disgust of Beethoven's followers—the program also included an aria from Rossini's opera *Tancredi*. But the spring weather was beautiful, and the hall was only half-full, reinforcing Beethoven's low opinion of the Viennese audience's seriousness about music. He spent much of the remainder of the year arranging for the symphony's publication elsewhere—especially in London—where, he hoped, its true worth might be better understood.

After those concerts in May of 1824, Beethoven left for his usual summer retreat to pleasanter places, this time the familiar Baden. (The move was probably not a simple matter, for his Broadwood grand piano came along.) While there, he received a visitor from London, the German-born manufacturer of harps and other musical instruments, Johann Andreas Stumpff. The two entertained each other at dinners, and Beethoven played for his guest on his English piano. Stumpff later recalled,

> Much of his talk was a criticism of the frivolity and poor musical taste of the Viennese. Beethoven had an exaggerated opinion of London and its highly-cultured inhabitants: "England stands high in culture. In London everybody knows something and knows it well; Viennese men can only talk of

eating and drinking; or they sing and pound away at music of little significance, often of their own making." He spoke of sending his nephew to London to make a man of him.

But the impulse for Beethoven's final major creative endeavor came from another direction. In the fall of 1822, a young Russian nobleman and cellist then residing in Vienna, Prince Nikolay Galitzin, had commissioned Beethoven to write "one, two, or three" string quartets. Beethoven promised three quartets, but postponed any work on them as he concentrated on the major compositions at hand. The first full performance of the *Missa solemnis* took place in St. Petersburg in April 1824. Now, with the huge labors of the *Missa* and the Ninth behind him, Beethoven turned toward that highly concentrated and much more intimate genre—and the focus of his attention during his final years—the string quartet.

9. Struggle and Culmination, 1825-1827

*C*ompositions discussed in the present chapter:

String Quartet, Op. 127

String Quartet, Op. 132

String Quartet, Op. 131

During 1825, three matters absorbed most of Beethoven's attention: the three Galitzin string quartets, his health, and concerns about Karl.

After those monumental creations of the early 1820s, the *Missa solemnis* and Ninth Symphony, he now turned his attention to that intimate and diminutive vessel, the string quartet. From now until his death, all his major compositions were quartets, and in these works, he revealed ever new and impressive facets of his late style.

In early January 1825, Beethoven offered the first of the Quartets commissioned by Nikolay Galitzin, Op. 127 in E♭, to his long-time associate, the violinist Ignaz Schuppanzigh and his quartet, for performance at a new series of concerts. Delighted, Schuppanzigh immediately announced in a newspaper advertisement that this premiere was to take place at the end of the month. But Beethoven had also offered the quartet to Joseph Linke (cellist in Schuppanzigh's quartet) for performance at his own concert about the same time. And, furthermore, the quartet was not finished. In the end, Schuppanzigh's group played this composition for the first time in March. But as Beethoven had given the music to him less than two weeks before the performance, the under-rehearsed piece went badly and made little impression.

When Beethoven learned about this—he was not present at the

concert—he persuaded Schuppanzigh's rival, Joseph Böhm, to perform the quartet with the other members of Schuppanzigh's quartet. Böhm described what happened:

> Neither objections nor doubts could prevail; what Beethoven wanted had to take place, so I undertook the difficult task. We studied it industriously and rehearsed it repeatedly under Beethoven's own eyes. And I mean Beethoven's *eyes*, for the unhappy man was so deaf that he could no longer hear the heavenly sound of his creations. But rehearsing in his presence was not easy. His eyes followed the bows closely so that he was able to judge the smallest fluctuations in tempo or rhythm and to correct them immediately.

After these preparations, Böhm led the group in four evidently successful performances. A local paper reported that "The Professor now performed this wonderful quartet twice over in a single evening for the same very numerous company of artists and connoisseurs in a way that left nothing to be desired; the misty veil disappeared, and the fine work of art radiated in all its dazzling glory."

In its overall shape, Op. 127 might look rather traditional: four movements in a usual sequence of slow introduction/fast; slow; scherzo/trio; fast. But the overall effect is anything but routine, starting with that slow introduction (Maestoso) that keeps returning intrusively during the first movement, always in a different key, and lending ever new colorings to its surroundings. The second movement is a theme and variations, that favorite vessel for the profound utterances of Beethoven's late period. As in the *Diabelli Variations*, a high level of abstraction from the theme begins with the first variation; later ones soar to the top of the strings' ranges, as we survey the endless implications Beethoven saw in that theme. The finale begins with a gesture Beethoven came to love in his late years: an imperious octave leap that commands our attention; even so, what follows shows us that we are in the wrong key and the *real* beginning is yet to come. Then the last part of this movement seems to peer into the future as we hear harmonies and motions we easily associate with Beethoven's much younger Viennese colleague, Franz Schubert.

New acquaintances and collaborators

In mid-1825, an important new Schindler-like figure entered Beethoven's life: the 26-year-old Karl Holz, a violinist in Joseph Böhm's string quartet (later also occasionally in Schuppanzigh's ensemble). At first, Beethoven employed him as a copyist, but gradually—as Schindler fell out of favor—began to use him as the sort of personal factotum that always seemed necessary for the conduct of Beethoven's daily life. One thing about Holz that Beethoven clearly appreciated was his name, which in German means "wood" or, sometimes, "the (wooden) cross of Christ." This fed into Beethoven's remorseless love of punning; his new friend routinely became "Holz Christi" or variations thereupon. Another attractive feature about Holz was his appreciation of wine and suitability as a dining-drinking companion. He described Beethoven's proclivities along those lines as follows:

> He was a stout eater of substantial foods; he drank a great deal of wine at table, but he could stand a great deal. Sometimes in merry company he became tipsy. In the evening he drank beer or wine, generally the wine of Vöslau [a wine center in Austria] or Hungarian red. When he had drunk he never composed.

In April of 1825, Beethoven suffered from digestive problems and remained indisposed for a month. His physician, one Dr. Anton Braunhofer, issued a stringent prohibition: no wine, coffee, or spices; he wrote in a conversation book: "Then I will guarantee you full recovery which means a lot to me, understandably, as your admirer and friend ... An illness does not disappear in a day. I shall not trouble you much longer with medicine, but you must adhere to the diet. You'll not starve on it."

During his illness, Beethoven received a young visitor from Berlin, the author—and later fearsome music critic—Ludwig Rellstab, who hoped to supply Beethoven with an opera libretto. But the composer cautioned him, "It must be something I can regard with sincerity and love. I could not compose operas like *Don Giovanni* and *Figaro*. They are repugnant to me. I would never have chosen such; they are too frivolous." Rellstab accordingly gave Beethoven a list of properly earnest subjects, among them Attila, Antigone, Belisarius, and Orestes. But as always in Beethoven's ongoing search for a new opera subject, nothing came of Rellstab's suggestions.

During a subsequent visit, Rellstab admired Beethoven's Broadwood piano, sent as a gift from its London maker.

> He turned to me, and seeing my eyes fixed upon the instrument he said, "That is a beautiful pianoforte. I got it as a present from London . . . and it has such a beautiful tone. He moved his hands to the keys without taking his eyes off me. He gently struck a chord . . . a C-major chord with his right hand and a B in the bass with his left, and, continuing to look uninterruptedly at me, repeated the false chord several times . . . and the greatest musician on earth did not hear the dissonance!

And during another visit from Rellstab, Beethoven held forth at length on one of his favorite subjects, the frivolous taste of the Viennese upper classes: "Since the Italians have gotten such a strong foothold here, the best has been crowded out. Among the nobility, the big thing at the theater is the ballet. Nothing can be said for their appreciation of art; all they care about is horses and dancers."

Exerting control over Karl

In early May, Beethoven felt sufficiently recovered to make his usual summer move, this time to his favorite warm-weather resort, Baden. There he wrote to his physician Braunhofer in Vienna, partly in jest, in the form of a dialogue:

D[octor]: How are you, my patient?

P[atient]: We are not so well—still feeling very weak, belching, etc. . . . Surely I might be allowed to drink white wine diluted with water . . . There can be no doubt that my stomach has dreadfully weakened, as has, generally speaking, my whole constitution.

D: I will help you, using partly the method of Brown, and partly that of Stoll [two famous physicians who advanced starkly opposed theories].

P: I would love to regain my strength so as to sit at my desk again . . . That last medicine I took only once, and then lost it.

He finished the letter with a brief musical canon—the sort of thing Beethoven often dashed off for friends—composed to the words, "Doctor, block the door to death; notes also help one out of need [Noth]."

Before long, Beethoven was indeed able to sit at his desk again and carry on with the Galitzin quartets. He resumed work on the second of them, Op. 132 in A minor, begun the previous February, finishing it in July. The work has five movements of which the central one had explicit personal significance: "Molto Adagio. Sacred Song of Thanksgiving to the Divinity by a Convalescent, in the Lydian mode. (The "Lydian mode" is a type of musical scale in ancient church music which—though rarely used—was associated with recovery and healing.) This movement begins with a sober, archaic-sounding hymn-like melody that seems to hover in the atmosphere. Beethoven then subjects this tune to a series of variations during which the music at points rises to heights of great emphasis and tension–tension relieved by more settled passages that Beethoven marks "feeling new strength."

During the earlier part of 1825, nephew Karl was ever more a source of unease. In 1824-5, he became increasingly dissatisfied with the course of philological studies he was pursuing at the University of Vienna; he finally persuaded his reluctant uncle that he should transfer to the Polytechnic Institute to prepare for a career in business. Beethoven was careful that during his own summer absence 19-year-old Karl, attending school in the city, was well surrounded by observant adults: he arranged that an official at the Institute be appointed as co-guardian, and that Karl move into the home of Beethoven's friend (and copyist), Matthias Schlemmer. Sundays and holidays, it was agreed, he was to travel to Baden to be with his uncle.

On week-days, Beethoven bombarded his nephew with messages, sometimes anxious, often trivial, which he now routinely signed with variations of "Your faithful father." On May 17, he wrote:

> The weather here is horrible. Today is even colder than yesterday, so that I can scarcely move my fingers to write . . . I forgot the chocolate today. I am sorry to trouble you with this. Doubtless all these difficulties will soon cease . . . If possible, send the chocolate by the afternoon mail coach, for, if not, I shall have none the day after tomorrow.

And the next day (in one of three notes that day):

> Don't worry. Study faithfully, and get up early in the morning. In this way you can even manage to do some things for me that might come up. It is surely a good thing for a youth of almost nineteen to combine the duties attendant to his own education with those he owes to his benefactor and supporter–as I certainly did with respect to my parents.

But a letter from late May has an utterly different tone; it shows in full force Beethoven's obsession with maintaining iron control over Karl, particularly to prevent any contact between him and his mother:

> So far only suppositions, though indeed someone assures me that you and your mother have again been meeting in secret. Am I to experience once more this abominable ingratitude? No, if the bond must be broken, so be it. But you will be despised by all impartial people who hear of such ingratitude . . . I have done my part, and can thus appear before the Supreme Judge of all judges. Don't be afraid to come to me tomorrow . . . So far I am only guessing. May God grant that nothing of this is true.

By the early fall, it was clear that Beethoven's new factotum, Karl Holz, had agreed to lend a hand in managing young Karl. Here are some of his entries in the Conversation Books:

> I have a plan to attach him closer to myself; perhaps I can win him over to my side; perhaps I can learn to know him and his way of life more easily.

> I have lured him into going to a beer house with me so I could see if he drinks too much; but that does not appear to be the case. Now I will invite him to play billiards; then I will see if he has already been practicing for a long time.

> I also told him that his uncle would be more inclined to give him money if he listened to some classic pieces at the Burgtheater a few times each month.

And a bit later, Beethoven wrote anxiously to Matthias Schlemmer, Karl's supervisor:

> One might be led to suspect that perhaps he really is enjoying himself in the evening or even at night in some company

which is clearly not so desirable—I request you to pay attention to this and not to let Karl leave your house at night under any pretext whatever, unless you have received something in writing from me through Karl.

Visitors in Baden and Vienna

During all this unease, in September 1825 Beethoven received a visitor from London, the distinguished conductor, organist, and founding member of the Philharmonic Society, Sir George Smart. He was one of Beethoven's most avid enthusiasts in England and had recently conducted the London premiere of the Ninth Symphony. His main reason for this visit, he said, was "to ascertain from Beethoven himself the exact times [tempos] of the movements of his characteristic [i.e. the Ninth]—and some of his other sinfonias." Smart and Beethoven first met at a hotel in Vienna where Karl Holz and members of the Schuppanzigh quartet played the recently completed String Quartet, Op. 132. Smart recorded in his journal:

> He received me in the most flattering manner. There was a numerous assembly of professors to hear Beethoven's second new manuscript quartette . . . This quartette is three-quarters of an hour long. They played it twice . . . It is most chromatic and there is a slow movement entitled "Praise for the recovery of an invalid." Beethoven intended to allude to himself, I suppose, for he was very ill during the early part of the year. He directed the performers, and took off his coat, the room being warm and crowded. A staccato passage not being expressed to the satisfaction of his eye, for alas, he could not hear, he seized Holz's violin and played the passage a quarter of a tone too flat.

Upon a later visit to Beethoven in Baden, Smart finally learned about tempos of the symphonic movements by persuading Beethoven to play them for him at the piano.

During his visit, Smart renewed the effort, previously pursued by Beethoven's younger colleagues in London, Ferdinand Ries and Charles Neate, to interest him in a trip to England. In a conversation book Karl recorded what Smart said (presumably in English):

> He said that in a short time you could easily make 1,000 pounds and take it away with you . . . And you'll gain 1,000 friends who will do anything to help you . . . In two years at least 50,000 florins net.

Beethoven, always an admirer of England and the English, chronically toyed with the idea of such a visit. But unlike his predecessor and teacher Haydn, who spent four memorable seasons there, he could never quite gather the resolve actually to make that trip.

In October, Beethoven moved from Baden to what was to be his final abode in Vienna, the second floor of the Schwarzspanierhaus ("black Spanish house," so named because it had been built by Spanish Benedictines). One benefit of this new abode was that his old friend from Bonn, Stephan von Breuning, lived nearby. The two now renewed their close relationship, which lasted until the composer's death. Beethoven had many meals at the Breunings' home, and, their daughter Marie reported, sometimes paid excessive attention to Stephan's wife; he confessed to her that he "longed greatly for domestic happiness and much regretted that he had never married." Beethoven also grew very fond of Breuning's 12-year-old son Gerard (he nicknamed him "trouserbutton" because he "stuck to his father as a button to trousers"). Much later Gerhard published a memoir, *Aus dem Schwarzspanierhaus*, that describes in fascinating detail the Breunings' association with Beethoven during his final years.

Another reminder of his long-vanished youth in Bonn came at the end of 1825 with a long and friendly letter from his old friend, the physician Franz Gerhard Wegeler. Addressing Beethoven as "My dear old Louis," he recounted recent events in his own life as well as news about the family of his wife, Eleonore von Breuning (once much beloved of Beethoven); Eleonore appended her own affectionate note to Wegeler's letter.

Toward the end of his letter Wegeler asks, "Why have you not avenged the honor of your mother, when in the *Conversations-Lexikon* and in France, they make you out to be a love-child?" He referred to claims in a chatty periodical from Leipzig, and in a French musical dictionary from 1810, that Beethoven was the illegitimate son of (one claimed) Friedrich Wilhelm I, King of Prussia (1688-1740), or (the other said) his successor Frederick the Great (1712-86). In his reply (after a year's delay) Beethoven wrote, "I have adopted the principle of neither writing anything about myself nor replying to anything written about me. Hence I gladly leave it to you to make known to the world the integrity of my parents, and especially of my mother." But speculations of this sort about Beethoven's possibly noble lineage persisted, and there is reason to suspect he was not altogether horrified by them.

Rehearsing the Galitzin quartets and stalled works

During the latter half of 1825 Beethoven's creative powers seemed fully restored; he finished the three Quartets for Galitzin, Op. 127 in E♭, Op. 132 in A minor, and Op. 130 in B♭ (in its first version). Beethoven's fellow musicians rushed to study and perform these difficult compositions—in some cases repeatedly—so that they became instantly known among Vienna's audience for such rather rarified music. This new surge in his visibility was likely a factor in the decision of the exclusive local Gesellschaft der Musikfreunde, a sponsor of concerts, a musical archive, and a conservatory, to, at last, elect Beethoven a member—the sort of honor he was always more than happy to receive.

Early in 1826, Beethoven fell ill again: with the same digestive difficulties, but also problems with his eyes, and, he reported a little later, with rheumatism. The redoubtable Dr. Braunhofer once more made his unwelcome recommendations: various proscriptions including no wine or coffee. By late February, Beethoven could write to his physician, "I am extremely obliged to you for your attentive care for my health. So far as it has been at all possible, I have held to your recommendations: wine, coffee, everything according to your plan." Another sign in this letter of an improved state was a return of his old brand of humor: "I am extremely sorry not to be able to prescribe something for you in return, and must just leave you to your own devices."

During his illness, the Schuppanzigh Quartet rehearsed the last of the three Galitzin quartets, i.e. Op. 130 in B♭, at Beethoven's home. Holz reported that the composer sat between the first and second violins, "for although he could no longer hear the low-pitched sounds, his ear still caught something of the higher sounds. Beethoven specified the tempos, the retards, and the like, and also demonstrated certain passages for us at the piano."

One of this quartet's six movements gave the group serious trouble, namely the redoubtable final fugue—an immensely complex, relentless structure nearly twice the length of the first movement. At the first performance of the quartet in March, the audience was delighted with some movements—particularly the slow Cavatina—and demanded their repetition; the gargantuan fugue evoked only bafflement. The efforts Beethoven's friends made to urge its replacement were to no avail until the publisher Artaria offered to publish the fugue separately—and pay Beethoven an additional fee. Thus, we have the redoubtable *Grosse Fuge*, Op. 133, as an independent composition. In its place, Beethoven later supplied the quartet with something as different as can be imagined: a cheerful Allegro dominated by an elfin, dance-like main theme.

During this period, when he composed little but string quartets, Beethoven surveyed the possibilities for continuing his creative work in other ways. Holz later recalled that Beethoven entertained expansive plans: "In the future I shall write in the manner of my grand-master Handel each year only an oratorio or a concerto for some string or wind instrument—provided that I have completed my tenth symphony (C minor) and my Requiem." Some friends urged him, in vain, to think again about his friend Karl Bernard's oratorio text, *The Victory of the Cross*, which he had already promised to set for the Gesellschaft der Musikfreunde. Another writer whom Beethoven saw a good deal in those days, Christoph Kuffner, persuaded him to compose an oratorio on the subject of the biblical King Saul; Kuffner quickly completed the first section of the libretto, but Beethoven never got around to that project either.

The director of the Imperial Court Theater expressed interest in a new Beethoven opera, suggesting Franz Grillparzer's tale of the elusive water-sprite Melusine—this, too, to no avail. One part of Beethoven's final grand plan did see some progress: he left rather substantial sketches for a tenth symphony. Holz even reported that he "played the Tenth Symphony in its entirety at the piano. He left some sketches for all its movements, but no one else could decipher them." An attempt by one modern musician to reconstruct the symphony from those sketches has met with considerable disbelief; the work has remained something of a tantalizing ghost.

Final works

And, as it turned out, there was to be no new opera or oratorio either. The only pieces of any scope Beethoven produced during his final months were two more string quartets, Op. 131 in C# minor, completed in July 1826, and Op. 135 in F major, finished the following October. The latter quartet is an impressive work of modest proportions. After a splendidly calm, slow movement (Lento assai, cantante e tranquillo, i.e., "very slow, singing, tranquil"), Beethoven inserts into the score some puzzling snatches of melody with words added: "Must it be? It must be! It must be!" (In performance, quartets generally ignore this insertion). From these few notes, Beethoven constructed a leisurely finale with—at some level—words and their meanings attached.

Some have concluded, not unreasonably, that in the last piece Beethoven ever composed, he addressed some matter of serious, maybe existential import: resignation and acceptance, perhaps, as life draws to an end. But the actual explanation, it seems, is rather more prosaic. Beethoven's friend, the music patron Ignaz Dembscher, wished to have the Quartet Op. 133 (with the *Grosse Fuge* still attached) performed at his home. Holz, at Beethoven's instruction, told him he could not have the score because he had not attended the performances of Schuppanzigh's quartet; his only recourse was to send Schuppanzigh the subscription price of 50 ducats. Dembscher, Holz reported, asked "Must it be?" to which Holz duly replied, "It must be." Upon hearing about this exchange, Beethoven, much amused, immediately wrote out a canon on those words—and later incorporated it into his final work. In this quartet, as so often happens, we see Beethoven operating on utterly diverse levels, invoking at once the exalted and the earthy.

The String Quartet in C# minor, Op. 131, which Beethoven once called his finest composition, is another in the remarkable series of masterpieces of his last years. According to the composer's own numbering, it has, on the face of it, seven movements—with no pauses between them. But we soon see that No. 3 serves as a brief introduction to the spacious theme-and-variations that follows, and No. 6 serves the same function for the finale. That leaves five ostensibly independent movements of which three conform to the usual pattern of a sonata-type composition: a "slow movement" (no. 4), a scherzo (no. 5), and a finale (no. 7) with some resemblance to a rondo.

But the quartet opens, remarkably, with a solemn fugue—dead serious but more compact and accessible than the *Grosse Fuge*—that evokes that central figure in Beethoven's musical upbringing, J. S. Bach (its main theme bears a familial resemblance to that of Bach's monumental *Art of the Fugue*). The following movement, innocent and idyllic, comes without pause as a comforting sequel (or, perhaps, antidote) to the severity of the fugue. Movement no. 3, as we have said, serves an introductory function, and it does so in a very special way. Its peremptory opening chords, followed by a meandering first violin line, remind us of "accompanied recitative"–those moments of high drama in opera or oratorio where stern, domineering orchestral interjections accompany and often interrupt, an agitated singer.

Recitative, of whatever sort, nearly always serves as an introduction to aria; here the "aria" is the fourth movement, a spacious, wonderfully diverse theme-and-variations, the central building block of this quartet. Its theme, lilting and innocent, comes in two halves, each repeated. Next come six astonishingly inventive variations on that theme, as if there is no limit to the implications Beethoven can draw from such a modest beginning. At points (as in the fourth variation), he exploits the ranges of the instruments to their utmost, driving the cello far up into the violin range to produce a strained, ghostly sound–leading us inevitably to wonder if this is really the effect its deaf creator imagined.

Of all the variations, the sixth is the longest because of its slow tempo. Its first section provides a placid, hymn-like fulcrum for the entire quartet, a release, for the moment, from all the rhythmic vigor and dynamic extremes that govern this composition. The close of the movement plays upon the lofty sound of the theme's ending, and the movement comes full circle to the serenity with which it had begun.

Problems with Karl

For some 30 years, Beethoven had spent the summer months in pleasant country places where he could work in peace during the long days. But in the summer of 1826, he hesitated, vacillated, and finally went nowhere. A reason lies close at hand: summer retreats meant distance from Karl and, hence, loss of control. (Beethoven had recently taken to waiting at the Polytechnic Institute at the noon recess in order to escort his nephew home arm-in-arm.)

At the end of July, just as Beethoven finished the Quartet Op. 131, Karl disappeared. The landlord Schlemmer reported, ominously, that he had discovered loaded pistols in Karl's room and confiscated them. When Holz, whom Beethoven dispatched to search for Karl, found him at the Polytechnic Institute, the youth said, "What good will it do you to detain me? If I do not escape today, I will another time." But he did escape from Holz that day; afraid to return to his home, he pawned his watch, bought two more pistols with powder and balls, and made his way to Baden. There he wrote letters (now lost) to Beethoven and a friend, climbed to the top of a rise in the Helenenthal—the valley, ironically, where Beethoven had so loved to walk—aimed the pistols in turn at his left temple, and fired. The first shot missed entirely; the second bullet lodged in his scalp, creating a flesh wound. A passing workman, apparently at Karl's request, took him to his mother's house in Vienna.

The usual explanation of this outcome has been that Karl failed to kill himself because of ineptitude with firearms. But aiming a pistol accurately at one's head seems a fairly straightforward matter, and modern psychology would likely interpret this event otherwise: at some level, Karl meant not to kill himself, but to call attention to his distress—this was a cry for help. In time, he gave somewhat differing explanations for his action. But mainly they centered around his relationship with Beethoven, to whom Holz reported: "He said he was tired of life, because he wanted from it something other than what you could approve." He also mentioned "Weariness of imprisonment," and being "tormented too much" by his uncle.

Overcoming his aversion to Karl's mother, Beethoven hurried to his bedside, where Karl wrote in a conversation book, "Do not plague me with reproaches and lamentations; it is past. Later all may be worked out." Beethoven wrote a desperate note to the physician Carl von Smetana: "A great misfortune has happened, a misfortune that Karl has accidently brought upon himself . . . Karl has a bullet in his head. How this has happened you will learn in due course—But come quickly, for God's sake, quickly." Smetana seemed hesitant to get involved, perhaps because under Austrian law attempted suicide was a crime. After another physician treated Karl, the police took charge and removed him for an extended stay at the city's General Hospital, where his prescribed treatment included religious instruction (administered by a Redemptorist), as the law prescribed for all who attempted suicide.

Gerhard von Breuning described Beethoven's reaction (one clearly tinged with self-centeredness) to this disaster:

> The pain he felt at this event was indescribable; he was crushed, like a father who has lost his beloved son. My mother bumped into him on the Glacis; he was completely unnerved, "Do you know what has happened to me? My Karl shot himself!"–"And–is he dead?" "No, he only grazed himself, he is still alive, there is hope that he can be saved–but the disgrace that he has caused me; I loved him so much!"

Still, Beethoven was good at compartmentalizing his life. Two days after this catastrophe, he was able to write a long and detailed letter to the director of the court theater at Mannheim about a performance of August von Kotzebue's play *The Ruins of Athens* that included his incidental music. The letter's only possible allusion to the drama unfolding around him is vague in the extreme: "As I have been overwhelmed with work, my reply is arriving rather late." And shortly thereafter, we see him much engaged with the question of the dedication of the Ninth Symphony (it ultimately went to the King of Prussia, whose return gift, a fake diamond ring, angered Beethoven and his friends).

As Karl lay in the hospital, Beethoven and friends held serious discussions about his future; a majority felt the best place for him would be the army. Karl, ever articulate, wrote in a conversation book: "If my wish about a military career can be fulfilled, I will be very pleased . . . So I ask you to employ the means you think best, and above all to see to it after my recovery that I get away from here as soon as possible."

Karl did leave Vienna almost immediately upon his discharge from the hospital in late September. But he did not join the army. Instead, Beethoven had accepted an invitation from his brother Johann to stay with Karl for a time at Johann's estate in Gneixendorf, a picturesque rural retreat about 40 miles west of Vienna with splendid views of the Danube valley. Beethoven and Karl set off on September 28 and arrived at Gneixendorf two days later. Here, for a reasonable rent, Johann provided them four spacious rooms and an attentive servant. In a letter to his publisher and friend, Johann Schott, Beethoven wrote (after giving meticulous metronome markings for all the sub-sections of the Ninth Symphony): "The district where I am now staying somewhat reminds me of the Rhine country which I so ardently wish to revisit."

At Gneixendorf, Beethoven fell into a well-defined schedule: rising at 5:30 AM, he composed at a table (while beating time with his hands and feet) until breakfast at 7:00. In both mornings and afternoons, he walked and sketched music in the open fields. His habit of shouting and gesticulating alarmed other residents, and once reportedly induced a team of oxen to bolt. But gradually, the stocky, square-ish figure striding along became familiar in these environs just as it was in the streets of Vienna.

While at his brother's estate, Beethoven composed the substitute movement for the *Grosse Fuge* and completed his final composition, the String Quartet in F, Op. 135. But these were also trying times, as his digestive woes returned with a vengeance. According to Johann, Beethoven's usual remedy for this problem was to drink more wine; "thereby his belly became bigger and bigger, and he wore a bandage over it for a long time." And conversation books suggest how things were going with his nephew and brother. Karl wrote:

> I beg of you once more not to torment me as you are doing; you might regret it. For I can endure much, but there are limits to what I can stand. You treated your brother the same way today without cause. You must remember that other people are human beings too.

Johann argued—in a letter, to avoid the tensions of direct confrontation—that Karl was wasting his time; he should return to Vienna and take his place in the military. Karl objected that the wound from "what happened to me" was still visible. But on a cold day at the beginning of December, two months after they had arrived, the ailing Beethoven and his nephew set off for Vienna in the only conveyance available, an open carriage.

Last illness

After a miserable trip, including an overnight stay in an unheated room in a village tavern, the two arrived at Beethoven's abode in Vienna, the Schwarzspanierhaus. Beethoven immediately took to his bed, and—after two physicians, perhaps not wishing to preside over a patient's death, declined to see him—a certain Dr. Wawruch from the Vienna General Hospital became a daily visitor. He first treated the composer for "inflammation of the lungs," but a week later found him "jaundiced all over his body. A frightful choleric attack had threatened his life . . . Trembling and shivering, he bent double because of the pains which raged in his liver and intestines, and his feet, thitherto moderately inflated, were tremendously swollen." He said an "enormous volume of liquid" had collected in his peritoneum (a condition now known as ascites). The treatment for it involved tapping—cutting an opening into the patient's abdomen. On December 20, a surgeon performed that operation in Beethoven's own bed. Beethoven exclaimed to the surgeon: "You remind me of Moses striking the rock with his staff!"

That month, Beethoven was cheered by the arrival of an impressive gift from Andreas Stumpff, harp manufacturer in London: the new 40-volume English edition in quarto of Handel's works. He exclaimed to young Gerhard von Breuning, "Handel is the greatest, the ablest composer; I can still learn from him." Gerhard went on, "He leafed through one volume after another as I gave them to him, sometimes stopping at particular passages, and then put one volume after another to his right on his bed up against the wall, finally making a heap that remained there for hours."

But the downward path of Beethoven's condition was inexorable; on January 8, he underwent a second operation to remove excess fluid. He was growing disenchanted with Dr. Wawruch, and a few days later several physicians, including Beethoven's one-time (but long estranged) friend Johann Malfatti, met to discuss the situation. Malfatti now effectively took over the case, and prescribed for Beethoven "nothing hereafter but frozen fruit punch and rubbing of the abdomen with ice-cold water." They also tried "sweat baths," in which Beethoven sat, covered with a sheet, above jugs of hot water. But he had other palliative care in mind. In February, he wrote to his publisher Schott in Mainz about the dedication of the Quartet Op. 131, appending a dubious, but "very important request—My doctor has prescribed for me some very good old Rhine wine . . . So if I could have a small number of bottles . . ."

When news of Beethoven's desperate condition reached London, the directors of the Philharmonic society voted to dispatch 100 pounds—1,000 florins in Beethoven's currency, a substantial sum—to ease any financial woes. Friends and admirers began to gather: his brother Johann, Holz, Schindler, and the two von Breunings were regularly at his bedside. (Nephew Karl, now in the military and stationed far to the east, never saw his uncle again.) Karl Bernard, Count Moritz Lichnowsky, and Andreas Streicher visited, as did a good many musicians, including Ignaz Schuppanzigh and Franz Clement. An unexpected visitor was the renowned pianist and composer Johann Nepomuk Hummel from Weimar; he arrived with his wife, who wiped the perspiration from Beethoven's brow, and his pupil Ferdinand Hiller, who would become a leading light in European music of the next generation.

A third and fourth operation followed, and gradually Beethoven's physicians began to see that a disease of the liver was the main culprit. But concluding that a cure was no longer possible, they lifted all restrictions. Friends—Streicher, von Breuning, his old landlord

Baron Pasqualati, as well as Dr. Malfatti himself—showered him with wine and food. And Beethoven had his preferences; in one of several notes to Pasqualati he wrote:

> Please send me some more stewed cherries today, but cooked quite simply, without any lemon. Further, a light pudding, almost like gruel, would give me great pleasure. My cook is not yet competent to provide me with an invalid diet. I am allowed to drink champagne: but please send me a champagne glass . . . Now about wine . . .

"Comoedia finita est"

During the latter part of Beethoven's career in Vienna, the younger composer Franz Schubert had increasingly gained recognition in the city. While Schubert was in awe of Beethoven—whom, by his own testimony, he had never met in person—Beethoven seems to have been barely aware of him. But Schindler reports that he brought a number of Schubert's songs to Beethoven on his deathbed. "For several days he could not separate himself from them, and every day he spent hours with 'Iphigenia,' 'Grenzen der Menschheit,' 'Die Allmacht,' 'Die junge Nonne' . . . With joyous enthusiasm he cried out repeatedly: 'truly a divine spark dwells in this Schubert!'" Some, including at least one Schubert scholar, have doubted the reliability of Schindler's report. But the later reminiscences of another close associate from that time, Anselm Hüttenbrenner, confirm it.

On March 23 the elder von Breuning drafted a will based upon an earlier note of Beethoven's, specifying that Karl was to be the sole beneficiary of his estate. Beethoven copied and signed the document with great difficulty, along with another one transferring the guardianship of Karl to von Breuning. That same day, according to Schindler and the younger von Breuning, as Beethoven's physicians were leaving his bedside, he exclaimed, in his "sarcastic-humorous manner, 'Plaudite amici, comoedia finita est.'" ["Applaud, friends, the comedy is finished."]. At the urging of his friends, Beethoven, a seriously lapsed Catholic, agreed to receive the last rites from a visiting priest, and died on the afternoon of March 26, 1827.

An autopsy, performed immediately, showed a variety of ailments; most serious was the condition of Beethoven's liver, "shrunk up to half its proper volume, of a leathery consistence and greenish-blue in color, and beset with knots . . ." Several medical evaluations have concluded that the cause of death was likely cirrhosis of the liver, perhaps associated with excessive drinking.

Beethoven's funeral took place on March 29. There was a preliminary service with singing in the courtyard of the Schwarzspanierhaus, as huge crowds jostled to gain entrance. Then a throng estimated at 10 to 20 thousand persons accompanied a procession, with the singers now serving as pallbearers, to the Trinity Church of the Minorites, where Beethoven's body entered a place of worship for the first time in many years. Several dozen musicians of the city, including Franz Schubert, served as torchbearers. After a ceremony in the church, a carriage took the body to the neighboring village of Währing, where, after an oration delivered in the parish churchyard by a noted tragedian, the body was lowered into its grave.

Cultural hero

Beethoven was far and away the most famous composer of his period. In fact, he achieved a degree of celebrity unmatched by any composer—or, likely, any artist—up to his time. For much of his adult life, his music routinely commanded high prices from aristocratic patrons, and increasingly from music publishers in several countries. His orchestral works were an outsized presence at concerts everywhere in Europe except France (where music-lovers were suspicious of anything foreign other than Italian opera).

One factor in Beethoven's success was this: he came along at a good time. During the later 18th century, Europe—particularly western Europe—saw an enormous growth in industry and trade that gradually transferred wealth and prestige from the old aristocracy to a burgeoning new class of industrialists, bankers, and—in greatest numbers—small merchants. From this movement arose that potent new social construct, a middle class (the term first appeared around 1812). This part of the population increasingly supported public musical performances and demanded those essential accouterments of amateur music-making at home: musical instruments and published scores. Beethoven adapted nimbly to this social shift, taking care to maintain his lucrative aristocratic connections as he addressed his efforts more and more toward the new public market. His symphonies and concertos became standard concert fare, while everywhere on the continent amateur musicians, both aristocratic and plebeian, played his sonatas and chamber music at home.

Especially in his later career, Beethoven wrote music mainly in genres that were going out of style. He continued to produce weighty symphonies and sonatas as most composers devoted their attention either to opera or to shorter character pieces, dances, and songs. But powerful new intellectual currents in the early decades of the 19th century, particularly in Germany, favored Beethoven's sort of music. Early romantic writers such as Jean Paul, Wilhelm Heinrich Wackenroder, and, particularly, E. T. A. Hoffmann, now placed instrumental music at the summit in their pantheon of the arts. And they did so precisely because of that which had always been considered music's deficiency: the conspicuous absence of a *subject*, of any clear connection with words, ideas, events, or scenes. For those writers, music referred not to things in this visible world, but to something beyond, something far loftier. And the prize exhibit in their reordered estimation of the arts was the instrumental music of Beethoven.

Such an exalted view of Beethoven's accomplishment lasted throughout the 19th century and beyond. This is not to say, however, that Beethoven's music was *popular* in the sense that his younger colleague Rossini's operas were. Beginning with the first works of his maturity, shortly after 1800, his music evoked from some quarters a litany of exasperated criticism: his pieces were too long, difficult, obscure, and eccentric. A critic had this to say about a private concert of 1804:

> Beethoven's symphony in C major [the First Symphony] was performed at Herr Würth's with precision and ease. A splendid artistic production . . . in which an uncommon richness of beautiful ideas are charmingly and splendidly developed. Overall there pervades continuity, order, and light. An entirely new symphony by Beethoven [the *Eroica*] is written in a completely different style. This long composition, extremely difficult of performance, is in reality a greatly expanded daring, wild fantasia . . . the reviewer belongs to Herr van Beethoven's sincerest admirers, but in this composition he must confess that he finds too much that is glaring and bizarre.

And this from an 1824 review of the Piano Sonata, Op. 111:

> Perhaps you, dear editor, can establish a position from which criticism and the commonly accepted rules of aesthetics can be defended against these novelties, these attacks on first principles. For when the primary conception of a work of art is divorced from reason, when feeling alone provides the basis for judgment, when works that scorn all our rules gain such passionate admirers—then I must be silent.

If Beethoven deviated ever more from rule and fashion, this seemed to detract not at all from the devotion of his admirers or the authority of his oeuvre. A paradox of the genuine masterpiece is that it must be in important ways *unique*—quite unlike other things of its kind—and, at the same time, *exemplary*, comprising a lasting standard of achievement, a model for others to emulate. Beethoven's instrumental works were seen as both for the entire 19th century and beyond. In the view of many, he held propriety rights for vast areas of composition: the symphony, the sonata, the string quartet, perhaps the piano concerto.

And the man himself—often suspicious and irascible but ultimately humane, increasingly a voluntary exile from society who seemed to follow inner lights of extraterrestrial origin—became a prototype for the romantic artist, a cultural hero from his time to our own.

10. Beethoven's Legacy

Beethoven's achievement became a nearly overwhelming presence in the minds of many European composers of following generations. One of these was Beethoven's admiring pall-bearer Franz Schubert, some 26 years younger than his idol, who practiced his art in the same city, unbeknownst to Beethoven until the very end of his life. But by the mid-1820s. Schubert had made himself well known in Vienna, mainly as a composer of "social music"–songs for one or more singers, dance music for piano or small ensemble. There was a ready local market for this kind of music, and Schubert published it in great profusion. His contributions to traditional instrumental fare–symphonies and ensemble or solo sonatas–tended in these years toward the lighter, more agreeable side.

Then, in the final half-dozen years or so of his life, and particularly after 1824, Schubert radically changed course. From then until his death in 1828, he devoted almost all of his energies–contrary to his own financial interests–to big, serious instrumental pieces, most of which remained unpublished during his lifetime. Thus we have that breath-taking succession of late works, including the "Unfinished" and "Great C-major" Symphonies, the String Quintet, a series of string quartets, two piano trios, and the three massive and marvelous piano sonatas from his final year. Schubert's motives for this drastic change in course are not very mysterious. In 1822, he had become seriously ill with a venereal disease, likely syphilis. Fearing that he had not long to live, and acutely aware of the disparity between his and Beethoven's profiles as composers, he plunged into a "Beethoven-project" (as a prominent Schubert scholar terms it): a last attempt to measure up to his hero, as best he could, by concentrating on Beethoven's sort of music.

After Schubert's death in 1828, Robert Schumann of Leipzig, in his role as a music critic, heralded Beethoven as a revolutionary and iconoclast who swept aside all artificial conventions, making way for the free expression of subjective musical values. Schumann and his coterie of fellow romantics saw in Beethoven the beginning of a new musical era–namely their own. As their opponents noted, there was nothing very remarkable about the young romantics' reverence for Beethoven's music in general: the symphonies were central to the repertory of every German orchestra, and every aspiring pianist did battle with the earlier sonatas. But Schumann and his journal were almost alone in championing Beethoven's little-appreciated late works. The Ninth Symphony and the late quartets and sonatas were, according to Schumann, Beethoven's highest achievements and ideal models for aspiring composers of his own generation.

But for Schumann the composer, the hovering specter of Beethoven's example alternately–and sometimes simultaneously–inspired and paralyzed. Schumann long took for granted that the real future for a romantic movement in music, founded by Beethoven, lay in the cultivation of Beethoven's kind of music: the large instrumental forms, especially the symphony. But, like many of his like-minded contemporaries, Schumann found this challenge unnerving: in his earlier career, he made periodic stabs at writing a symphony, but never quite managed to finish a movement.

During the 1830s, his first decade devoted to composition (after giving up on law school) Schumann produced a series of colorful, improvisatory-sounding short piano pieces; the year 1840 then saw a marvelous outpouring of solo songs. Schumann's music of the 1830s suggests that Beethoven was never far from his thoughts. Among recurrent subtle references to his great predecessor, a passage in the Fantasy Op. 17 (1836-8), for example, quotes a touching passage in Beethoven's song cycle "An die ferne Geliebte" ("To the Distant Beloved"). In 1841, at last, Schumann finished a symphony (named "The Spring"), and in the remaining 15 years of his life, he composed three more. He had finally overcome–or perhaps merely slipped past–the overwhelming challenge of Beethoven's example.

In France, always rather culturally isolated–and often proudly so—Beethoven remained something of a non-entity until the later 1820s. The French first noticed him just as they came to see some virtue in that other foreigner, long despised for his irregularities and excesses, William Shakespeare. As late as 1822, when an English troupe presented *Othello* in Paris, the audience hissed them off the stage; a projectile thrown from the pit wounded an actress (reportedly as she curtsied). But five years later, *Hamlet* and *Romeo and Juliet* played at the Odéon theater to a reasonably attentive audience—and to a claque of young romantics who cheered throughout.

The French got their first substantial dose of Beethoven in 1828 when Franz Habeneck conducted the Paris Conservatory Orchestra in a concert series devoted almost exclusively to his works. Noisy enthusiasm for this newly-discovered "untamed genius"—particularly among those same young romantics—grew by leaps and bounds. After a performance of the *Eroica*, a French critic inquired wistfully, "Why do we allow ourselves to be outdone by foreigners? How does it happen that this masterwork, which the Germans have known by heart for twenty years, should have been introduced here only last week?"

A rapt member of the audience for the performances of Shakespeare's plays in 1827 and Beethoven's works in 1828 was a mercurial young medical student-turned-composer, Hector Berlioz. Of *Hamlet*, he exclaimed in his Memoirs: "Shakespeare, coming upon me unawares, struck me like a thunderbolt. The lightning-flash of that discovery revealed to me at a stroke the whole heaven of art, illuminating it to its remotest corners." Berlioz had scarcely recovered from this encounter when he confronted Beethoven: "The shock was almost as great as that of Shakespeare had been. Beethoven opened before me a new world of music, as Shakespeare had revealed a new universe of poetry." Like Schumann, Berlioz long pursued a double career as composer and music critic, and in neither role was Beethoven ever far from his thoughts. In 1838, Berlioz published a series of devoted and detailed articles on the Beethoven symphonies. And relating that music to his own aspirations as a composer, he wrote, "Now that I have heard the terrifying giant

Beethoven, I know exactly where musical art stands; the question is to take it from there and push it further."

Beginning shortly after mid-century, the musical world of central Europe gradually divided into two ever more distinct factions. On one side was the "New German School," led by Wagner and Liszt, who held that music achieved its true effect only when joined with words and ideas—with poems, narratives, or scenes. Wagner argued extravagantly that there was no longer any need for the individual arts as such; all should simply be absorbed within the "great universal artwork of the future"—i.e. his own musical dramas such as the monumental cycle, *The Ring of the Nibelung*. On the other side, Schumann, Brahms, and other like-minded musicians believed in the continued viability of those sturdy old categories of instrumental music such as sonatas and symphonies.

Both factions remarkably looked to Beethoven as their founding father. On the Schumann-Brahms side, this fealty was explicit and hardly surprising. Like Schumann, Brahms long hesitated to tread on Beethoven's turf, once remarking to a musician friend, "I will never finish a symphony. You have no idea how it affects one's spirits to hear continuously the marching of a giant behind him." His First Symphony, which he began in 1855, finally saw the light of day in 1876.

But Wagner, too, idolized Beethoven. Despite all his claims of originality and singularity, he acknowledged Beethoven as the inspiration for his newly invented genre, the music drama. It was in the Ninth Symphony, he reflected, as Beethoven added text and singing to its finale, that his predecessor took the first decisive step toward Wagner's "artwork of the future."

Most prominent among musicians of the following generation to cultivate the Beethovenian tradition was Gustav Mahler (1860-1911), who held positions as a conductor in a series of Austro-German musical centers before settling in Vienna in 1897. Like Beethoven, he composed nine symphonies—three with texts and choral singing—and attempted a 10th. One often hears the grandest of them, the Eighth (1907), performed at festive occasions; it has become something of a modern-day counterpart of Beethoven's Ninth.

But Mahler's optimistic prediction that "In thirty or forty years, my symphonies will be played at concerts as often as Beethoven's are today" did not come to pass. And he himself contributed to that outcome: as a conductor, Mahler led performances of Beethoven's music—often while enduring the slights of an anti-Semitic press—throughout the Western world, including, in his last years, on the podium of the New York Philharmonic Orchestra.

Shortly after Mahler's death in 1911, the ravages of World War I—in which more than a million soldiers from Austro-Hungary alone died—nurtured a climate in which many European artists questioned the significance and value of their earlier work. A few sought to do something radically different, and a wide variety of "modernisms" followed. In Beethoven's Vienna, a group of composers led by Arnold Schönberg set out to banish the most basic constructive principle that had governed European music for three centuries—*tonality*, or *being in a key*. (The first two pitches of the melody "My Country 'tis of Thee," for example, establish its key.) The systematic alternative that Schönberg's group introduced, "twelve-tone," or "serial" composition, offered modernist composers one ready-made option for a couple of generations.

But within the musical culture of the 20th and 21st centuries, this and other modernisms have turned out to be more an addition than a substitution. A core repertory of classical music, with Beethoven as a central presence, has continued to dominate concert performances throughout the Western world. And in the later 1900s, it also gained a decisive foothold in the East. At China's leading music school, the Shanghai Conservatory, the present curriculum is about evenly divided between Eastern and Western music; students study the works of Beethoven there, just as they do at the Juilliard School in New York.

During the last years of his life, Beethoven was known and admired far beyond the world of music and music lovers; in Austria, Germany, and even England he became something of a cultural icon.

And after his death in 1827, his stock continued to rise. The celebration of the 75th anniversary of his birth in his native city of Bonn saw torchlight processions and artillery salutes, the building of a new Beethovenhalle where an audience one-and-a-half times the size of the town's population listened to performances of his works. Attending the festivities were many of Europe's most admired musicians (Berlioz, Liszt, Meyerbeer, Louis Spohr, Jenny Lind) and royal eminences such as King Friedrich Wilhelm IV of Prussia, and England's Queen Victoria with her consort Prince Albert.

A century later, both sides in World War II invoked Beethoven's music to whip up patriotic fervor. As the war ended, German radio announced Hitler's death to the solemn accompaniment of the Funeral March from the *Eroica*. Further into the 20th century, as the Berlin wall came down in 1989, the attendant celebrations featured Leonard Bernstein conducting the Ninth Symphony—with "Freude" (joy) in the choral finale changed to the more apposite "Freiheit" (freedom).

And Beethoven's music has even escaped the confines of our planet. The space probes, Voyagers 1 and 2, launched in 1978 and still moving about the outer fringes of our solar system, have onboard recordings of the Fifth Symphony (first movement) and the Cavatina from the String Quartet Op. 130—just in case any extra-terrestrial beings might care to listen.

Sources

Albrecht, Theodore, ed. and trans., *Letters to Beethoven and Other Correspondence*, 3 Vols. (Lincoln Neb.: University of Nebraska Press, 1996).

Anderson, Emily, trans., *The Letters of Beethoven*, 3 Vols. (London: Macmillan, 1961).

Brandenburg, Sieghard, ed., *Ludwig van Beethoven, Briefwechsel Gesamtausgabe*, 7 Vols. (Munich: G. Henle Verlag, 1996).

Burnham, Scott, *Beethoven Hero* (Princeton: Princeton University Press, 1995).

Dahlhaus, Carl, *Ludwig van Beethoven: Approaches to his Music*, trans. Mary Whittall (Oxford: Oxford University Press, 1991).

Forbes, Elliot, ed. and rev., *Thayer's Life of Beethoven*, 2 Vols. (Princeton: Princeton University Press, 1964).

Köhler, K.-H; Herre, G.; and Beck, D. eds., *Ludwig van Beethovens Konversationshefte*, 13 Vols. (Leipzig: Breitkopf & Härtel, 1968-93).

Lockwood, Lewis, *Beethoven: the Music and the Life* (New York: W. W. Norton, 2003).

Lockwood, Lewis, *Beethoven's Symphonies: An Artistic Vision* (New York: W.W. Norton, 2015).

Plantinga, Leon, *Beethoven's Concertos: History, Style, Performance* (New York: W. W. Norton, 1999).

Schiedermair, Ludwig, *Der junge Beethoven* (Leipzig: Quelle & Meyer, 1925).

Suggested Reading

Breuning, Gerhard von. *Memories of Beethoven*. Ed. M. Solomon. Trans. H. Mins and M. Solomon (Cambridge: Cambridge University Press, 1992). Gerhard von Breuning, son of a life-long friend of Beethoven's, records his vivid impressions of the composer in his last years: his appearance, his way of speaking—often with sarcasm—eating, walking about town, and working.

Dennis, David B. *Beethoven in German Politics, 1870-1989* (New Haven: Yale University Press, 1996). Dennis discusses the adoption of Beethoven—the man and his music—as a useful symbol for widely diverse political ideologies in Germany, extending from the birth of the nation in 1870 through the horrors of the two world wars to the reunification of the two Germanys in 1989.

DeNora, Tia, *Beethoven and the Construction of Genius: Musical Politics in Vienna, 1792-1803* (Berkeley: University of California Press, 1995). This is a sociological analysis of Beethoven's singular fame. Arguing that the notion of genius is a "social construction," DeNora emphasizes the role that Beethoven's background and connections—as opposed to his accomplishment—played in his success.

Schindler, Anton. *Beethoven as I Knew Him. A Biography*, ed. D. W. MacArdle; trans. C. S. Jolly (Chapel Hill: University of North Carolina Press, 1966). Schindler, Beethoven's close companion and amanuensis from about 1820 until the composer's death, gives a first-hand account of his life and work. He also engages in a good bit of falsification, much of it self-serving. In his notes, MacArdle makes a determined effort to separate the wheat from the chaff.

Solomon, Maynard, *Beethoven*. 2nd Edition (New York: Schirmer, 1998). In this comprehensive and readable biography, Solomon gives a leisurely interpretative account of Beethoven's life, often with a noticeable psychoanalytic coloring.

Solomon, Maynard, *Beethoven Essays* (Cambridge, Mass.: Harvard University Press, 1998). This is a series of informed and imaginative pieces—with a psychoanalytic bent—on aspects of Beethoven's life, nature, and work: What is the underlying intent of the Ninth symphony? How do Beethoven's works relate to his life? Who was the "Immortal Beloved?" The volume ends with an annotated translation of Beethoven's diary from 1812-18.

Sonneck, O. G., ed., *Beethoven. Impressions by his Contemporaries* (New York: Dover, 1967). First published in 1927, this collection includes selected reminiscences of Beethoven's early associates in Bonn and of his later ones in Vienna. It also offers a series of contemporary portraits, and ends with the poet Franz Grillparzer's funeral oration in English translation.

Walden, Edward. *Beethoven's Immortal Beloved: Solving the Mystery*. Lanham, MD.: Scarecrow Press, 2011. Thirty years after Maynard Solomon identified, to most people's satisfaction, the addressee of Beethoven's famous "Immortal Beloved" letter as Antonie Brentano, Walden makes a detailed argument that it was actually intended for Antonie's step-sister, the hyper-imaginative author Bettina Brentano von Arnim.

Wegeler, Franz, and Ries, Ferdinand. *Beethoven Remembered*. Trans. Fredrick Noonan. (Arlington VA: Great Ocean Publishers Inc., 1967). These are reminiscences, often intimate and judged to be mainly reliable, of a friend and a student. The physician Wegeler and the musician Ries knew Beethoven for his entire life and leave us a valuable glimpse of Beethoven's activities and relationships. This edition includes a translation of explanatory notes by the editor of the original German edition, Alfred C. Kalischer.

About the Author

Leon Plantinga is Professor Emeritus of Music at Yale University, where he taught from 1963 to 2005. His books include *Schumann As Critic* (1967), *Clementi: His Life and Music* (1977), *Romantic Music: A History of Musical Style in Nineteenth-Century Europe* (1984), which serves as a standard textbook in American universities, and *Beethoven's Concertos: History, Style, Performance* (1999). Prof. Plantinga has also written many articles and reviews on European music, ca. 1750-1900.

A Word from the Publisher

Thank you for reading *Simply Beethoven*!

If you enjoyed reading it, we would be grateful if you could help others discover and enjoy it too.

Please review it with your favorite book provider such as Amazon, BN, Kobo, Apple Books, or Goodreads, among others.

Again, thank you for your support and we look forward to offering you more great reads.

www.ingramcontent.com/pod-product-compliance
Lightning Source LLC
Chambersburg PA
CBHW030151100526
44592CB00009B/218